A TOBY IN THE LANE

A TOBY IN THE LANE

a history of London's EAST END markets

PAUL MORRIS

First published 2014

The History Press
The Mill, Brimscombe Port
Stroud, Gloucestershire, GL5 2QG
www.thehistorypress.co.uk

British Library Cataloguing in Publication Data.
A catalogue record for this book is available from the British Library.

ISBN 978 0 7524 6284 4

Typesetting and origination by The History Press
Manufacturing managed by Jellyfish Solution Ltd.
Printed and bonded in Malta by Gutenberg Press Ltd.

CONTENTS

ACKNOWLEDGEMENTS

I would like firstly to express my appreciation to my wife Penny, without whose support and patience this book would not have been written, and to Costa, Sarah and other family members, for their encouragement and help. Many market traders have shown thoughtful generosity and enthusiasm during the course of this project: in particular, Munir Ahmed, Charlie Burns, Joe Barnett, Nej Fehmi, George Ozpembe, Terry Dervish, Pat Thorpe, Denise Brown, Alan Langley, Byron Thane, George Gladwell and John Calcutt. In the text that follows, some names have been changed to protect identities.

I am grateful to the library staff at Bishopsgate Institute, particularly Stefan Dickers, and at Tower Hamlets Archives, particularly Malcolm Barr-Hamilton, for their kindness, generosity and expertise. Many thanks are also due to the staff of the Jewish Museum, the Museum of London and the London Metropolitan Archives, with whose help I gained a great many insights and much knowledge.

Numerous others have helped enormously, including David Saunders, Phil Maxwell, Eugene McConville and Stephen Watts, donating their time and effort to this book in the form of remarkable photographs and narratives. My thanks go also to my colleagues and employees at Tower Hamlets Council. Last but not least, I am grateful to Michelle Tilling at The History Press for endorsing the project in the first place.

PREFACE

'From poacher to gamekeeper'

Like many individuals in London I was not born in the capital, but came pursuing work, to explore and trial my ambitions. I was raised in the Lake District in Cumbria in exquisite rural surroundings that could be described as the antithesis to city life and, in particular, London. As a teenage lad, though, I had an early relationship with markets: my first job was working in the Cumbrian market town of Milnthorpe, assisting a market trader in setting up his shoe stall in the early hours of the morning before I went to school. I swiftly realised what a physically demanding job market trading was – and still is – but enjoyed the lively atmosphere and environment of the market. I had an additional job as a butcher's assistant, where I learnt the essentials of trade and business.

My reason for leaving the North, however, was not markets but my passion for art. Following my ambition to paint and study I gained a place at art school in Cardiff. After my graduation in 1991 the inevitable move was to London to seek work and pursue an art career, but it soon became apparent that my art 'career' would not support me financially, even though I enjoyed some exhibiting success.

While continuing to paint I searched for job opportunities. For a short time I worked for the British Museum, which helped to ignite a love for history, but I soon realised that Portobello market, which was close to where I lived in Harlesden, in north-west London, provided the ideal opportunity for work. So, like many new immigrants to the city, I started my first job as a market trader in one of the most famous street markets in London. My stall sold second-hand clothes (labelled 'designer' before the popularity of the current 'vintage' label) that I procured from an auction house in Tooting that sold on lost luggage from London Transport and British Airways. Lacking a vehicle, I would pay for a taxi to deliver me and three or four large sacks of clothes that I hoped would bring financial reward to the market.

I soon recalled that the life of a market trader was not an easy one, and making money was a lot harder than I had imagined. My business enterprise was flawed: with little money to finance the business, no vehicle and little help I was doomed to failure. Nevertheless, I enjoyed the experience: the sense of independence, alongside the lively banter and intoxicating atmosphere of a bustling market, never left me.

For a few years afterwards I worked in enforcement jobs, including in the parking sector, while continuing to pursue a creative art career. The job in parking was, of course, that of a traffic warden and, while I was grateful for the work, it was a thankless occupation, stressful and demoralising. When the opportunity came up to apply for a position as a market inspector in Tower Hamlets I jumped at the chance. From 1996, when I started the appointment as the new market inspector, or 'Toby', I have not looked back. The environment of the market, its history, its characters and its day-to-day drama are enticing and addictive. A few years into the role, during a discussion about my personal history with my new manager David Saunders, an ex-army officer, he exclaimed with delight that since I had once been a market trader but was now a market inspector I had made the transition 'from poacher to gamekeeper'.

This book presents a chronicle of two of the most significant markets of London, Brick Lane and Petticoat Lane, and their relationship with authority. The two markets are a 10-minute walk apart, lying in the heart of the East End between Aldgate and Bethnal Green, and their history is synonymous with the plight of the East End – its struggles with immigration and for social justice, its stoic endurance in difficult times and the contrast of present-day impending gentrification.

INTRODUCTION

London, in its first incarnation, was a trading post of the Roman Empire. The area was carefully chosen for its estuarine location, where the trade and distribution of goods could easily be maintained. In subsequent centuries, as London grew, street trading became its lifeblood, creating an unparalleled number of markets, each serving its own communities and each offering a different character.

In medieval times markets developed in popularity alongside fairs. The markets of Cheapside, Newgate and Smithfield strove to feed the ever-growing tastes of the London population, and it became apparent over time that markets required regulation. Laws were brought in not only to legalise the right to hold a market within a certain locality but also to protect the customer. The entitlement to hold a market was typically granted by a Royal Charter. Laws determining market hours were quite strict and those who traded outside market areas and times were heavily punished. Many of these regulations still have an influence today and, indeed, their principal aim of consumer protection is more relevant now than it has ever been.

Two momentous events in London's history, the plague of 1665 and the Great Fire of London of 1666, changed the appearance of the city forever. Citizens who lived in suburbs outside the city's gates were less affected by the latter event and, after a short period of time, there began a population explosion and property boom. The need for new trading areas became pressing as a result of an Act of Parliament of 1674 that banned street markets within the city walls and a growing populace in London's growing suburbs, and it was not long before Petticoat Lane, just outside the walls, became perhaps the most important new market in London. With increased industrialisation in subsequent years the development of Brick Lane began.

These neighbouring markets would develop into the most famous street markets in London and, later, the world. They have been a cornerstone of London's culture for over 400 years and continue to occupy a prominent place in the landscape and, indeed, in our aspirations and dreams. This book is about these two most important markets of London, both situated in the heart of the East End and within half a mile of each other. Petticoat Lane and Brick Lane are monuments to the culture of the city: they represent its beating heart that has kept its lifeblood flowing for generations. A city is as much about its people as its historical buildings, great paintings or museum artefacts, and there are no places more fascinating in London's journey than these two markets, which have embodied so many different generations of London's communities in all their aspects: hopes and struggles, riches and poverty, humour and sorrow, crime and degradation.

Bewildered as to why these markets had been largely excluded from history, like an unturned rock in a pool, I felt compelled to tell their story. The rich underbelly of life that they represent is an almost forgotten strand to London's culture. John Marriott, in his book *Beyond the Tower*, describes Petticoat Lane as colourful, but notes that its 'origins … are lost in time'. Although there are inevitably elements missing from the history, in this book I will trace as far as possible the rich historical narrative of the markets and bring to life their contemporary tale.

During my work within the markets as an official of the council, as a market inspector, or Toby, their varied and vibrant life has enthralled me. The tales of traders in the arena of the marketplace past and present are extraordinary. Often they are of a good-humoured nature, sometimes crude and explicit, sometimes sombre and affecting, but together they sum up the history of London's immigrants over the many generations that have helped build the city, starting and making their lives within the markets of Petticoat Lane and Brick Lane.

These marketplaces have frequently been battlegrounds in which the radical, left-wing politics of the East End has been played out. They have seen the demands for better living conditions for impoverished immigrant communities; the rise of organised labour, where market traders formed their own organisations in a close reflection of the labour movement; and, of course, the battles between fascism and democracy.

In this book I will explore these themes, as well as the markets' contemporary issues. The markets are now possibly facing their greatest ever challenge for survival as they pit themselves against the gleam and spit of modern shopping centres, parking challenges and gentrification – they are fighting to be a truly meaningful part of twenty-first-century London.

Paul Morris, 2014

1

THE ORIGINS OF PETTICOAT LANE

Petticoat Lane could once, justifiably, be called 'world-famous'. Nearly twenty years ago, when I first encountered it, this was still the case. Now, however, it is somewhat diminished from that earlier status: such an assertion today seems an outdated claim to grandeur, given its present-day modest size and appearance. It remains a prominent feature of market life in London, however, and its history represents the very fabric and growth of London's development, mirroring the enormous population explosion and expansion of one of the world's greatest cities.

The history of the East End is inextricably tied up with its markets. Ancient markets such as Eastchepe have long since disappeared but Spitalfields, Roman Road, Bethnal Green, Watney Market, Chrisp Street, Columbia Road, Whitechapel and, of course, Brick Lane and Petticoat Lane very much continue to prosper, and it is evident that street trading has been instrumental to the development of the East End.

Hogge Lane

The earliest available historical references to the street now known as Petticoat Lane call it Berewards Lane. Berewards

Lane dates back to at least 1218, when it was a track leading from
Aldgate through fields to Bishopsgate and served as a shortcut to
the Whitechapel Essex Road. It was located close to the walled
City of London and as a consequence served as a popular route for
farmers and visitors making their way to 'Chepe' markets within
the city walls. Travellers often arrived too late at night, beyond the
curfew bells, to be admitted to the city, and Berewards Lane thus
became a convenient resting place.

The name Berewards Lane lasted until 1500, when it and land
adjoining were sold by its monastic owners to farmers, who used
it for the rearing of pigs. In John Stow's survey of London in 1598
he notes the change of name that resulted, from 'Berwards [sic]
Lane ... of olde time so called, but now Hogge lane'. Stow refers
extensively to it in his survey:

> This Hogge lane stretcheth North toward Saint *Marie Spitle* without
> Bishopsgate, and within these fortie yeares, had on both sides fayre
> hedgerowes of Elme trees, with Bridges and easie stiles to passe ouer
> into the pleasant fieldes, very commodious for Citizens therein to
> walke, shoote, and otherwise to recreate and refresh their dulled
> spirites in the sweete and wholesome ayre, which is nowe within few
> yeares made a continuall building throughout, of Garden houses,
> and small Cottages; and the fields on either side be turned into
> Garden plottes, teynter yardes, Bowling Allyes, and such like, from
> Houndes ditch in the West, so farre as white Chappell, and further
> towards the East.

The pig farming proved particularly successful, as its close
proximity to the food market of Eastcheap (distinguished from
Cheapside, which was in the west of the city) meant that fresh
meat could be easily transported out to customers, giving an
advantage over traders from further afield. As the pig-rearing
enterprises flourished they began to attract other tradesmen and
craftsmen to the area, developing the vicinity into an important
area for commerce. Such places were increasingly important

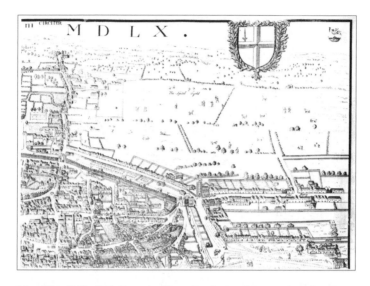

Map of Spitalfields, 1560. (Courtesy of Tower Hamlets Local History Library & Archives)

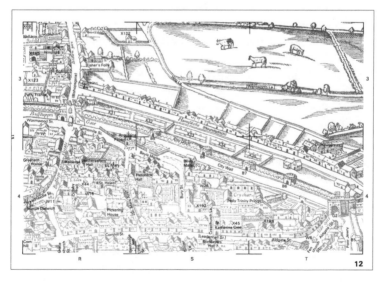

Elizabethan map. (Courtesy of Tower Hamlets Local History Library & Archives)

for the growing city. The population within the city walls by the year 1500 was no more than 75,000, the Black Death and other plagues having limited population growth, but during the next century expansion was enormous and by 1600 London's populace was 400,000. Parishes outside the city walls, such as Whitechapel and Shoreditch, underwent enormous increases in population, providing a spur to the development of the nascent markets.

The development of Spitalfields

After Henry VIII's break with Rome in the mid-sixteenth century land owned by monasteries and abbeys became available to lease for property speculators. The area later known as Spitalfields, after the hospital of St Mary of Spittal, which during the medieval period had catered for the sick and the poor, would come to play an important part in the expansion of the markets of Petticoat Lane and Brick Lane, and the surrounding area.

The significance of Spitalfields' association with Petticoat Lane cannot be underestimated. Spitalfields market was granted a licence by Charles I in 1638 but deteriorated until 1682, when Charles II granted a Royal Charter to John Balch, a silk thrower who married Katherine Wheeler, daughter of market trustee William Wheeler,[1] giving Balch the right to hold a market on Thursdays and Saturdays in the area of Spitalfields or its close proximity. This development was in response, of course, to the need to feed an ever-growing population in the area. Unfortunately John Balch died a year later and did not see his plans develop, but, fortunately for the future

---

1   A street in the area running from Commercial Street to Bethnal Green Road was named Wheeler Street. It was once an important location for illegal street trading until the extension of the East London railway line was built. Tower Hamlets Council recently changed its name to Braithwaite Street to coincide with this development. There is a sense here of the market's origins being slowly erased, both geographically and physically.

development of the area, he left the leasehold and market franchise to Edward Metcalf, who wasted no time in creating a permanent building to be used for market purposes.

Soon after the market was established Metcalf also unfortunately died and the lease was taken over by a trader from the City of London named George Bohun, who saw the potential in supplying the increasing population of the city with fresh fruit, vegetables and meat. The market soon became imperative to the stability of the community and was, indeed, London's most significant fruit and vegetable market at this time.

By the early 1700s the market was thriving and would soon be home to the area's second wave of immigration, the French Huguenots, who had fled France following religious persecution. French Huguenots, who were Protestants, had enjoyed the protection of their civil rights under the Edict of Nantes but these freedoms were repealed by Louis XIV, who tried to force conversion through repression. Up to 50,000 people fled as a result and came to London. It was at this time that the French word 'refugee' entered the English language.

The Huguenots were attracted to the area of Spitalfields because it had already been settled, over a century earlier, by Dutch and French silk weavers who had taken advantage of the area's close proximity to the city to expand their trade. The existence of a familiar and sympathetic community enticed the new wave of French Protestants, of whom a large majority practiced silk weaving. The silk weavers would tenter out their wet silk by means of hooks to prevent shrinkage in the spittal fields, giving the area a distinct identity. We are reminded of their presence today in so many ways and their influence upon the vicinity of Spitalfields cannot be understated – from houses built at the time (for example, in Fournier Street, Folgate Street, Princelet Street and Fashion Street, now the residences of artists such as Gilbert and George) to the language of the Huguenots, which has left its physical imprint on the area in place names such as Tenter Lane, which still leads from Spitalfields market. Indeed, at this time the area was known as Petty France. Their skills and expertise in silk weaving, alongside other trades and interest in arts, made the Huguenots into a distinct and successful community. They also engaged in many intellectual pursuits: historical and mathematical societies and interests in botany and music were very popular.

The Huguenots would soon be put under enormous pressure, however, when Irish immigrants began to arrive in the mid-1700s. Not only were these new settlers adept at weaving, but they were able to undercut the Huguenots in terms of wages and conditions of work, making cheaper alternatives. Tensions grew between the communities, culminating in riots in 1736 during which Irish businesses and homes were attacked by the Huguenots. Poor relations, poverty and a disgruntled workforce continued for many years until, in 1762, the Huguenot journeymen agreed a set of wage and work standards with their masters in an attempt to secure living wages. However, these standards were again undercut and renewed disorder characterised the period from 1769 to the mid-1770s. Peace finally broke out in 1773 when the first Spitalfields Act was passed to regulate working conditions and wages.

Although there was relative calm thereafter, the weavers' industry had gone into decline, partially as a consequence of the workings of the Spitalfields Acts, which were repealed in 1824. Subsequently attempts were made to preserve the silk-weaving industry, with a few companies remaining in the area. As late as 1900 an employee of one of these companies, George Dorcee, attempted to support the industry by appealing to the local authority against the demolition of weavers' houses. Incredibly, he succeeded, prolonging the industry for a few more years, but, perhaps more significantly for the area, also preserving its homes. By this time, however, the decline was terminal, leaving many weavers in poverty, and the Huguenot community was dispersed. Many weavers sought new employment within the docks or became market traders in the growing areas of Petticoat Lane and, ironically, the food market that had been established around the Spitalfields hospital site.

The impact of this food market in the area may often be understated but was in fact enormous. It served not only the Huguenot community but also the traders and costermongers of Petticoat Lane for over 200 years. Initially trading was conducted from a collection of sheds and stalls but, with London's growing appetite for fresh fruit and vegetables, it was in desperate need of modernisation by the mid-1800s. The market in its present form was finally rebuilt by former market porter Robert Hormer in 1888 after he had purchased the lease two years earlier and was run by the City of London; it then continued to serve for another 100 years as a wholesale fruit and vegetable market. Wholesale trade at Spitalfields ceased in 1991, after which it was left unused until redevelopment in 2005. The market was fully restored in 2008, with a Norman Foster-designed office block at its western end. It is now a beacon for artisan trade and plays an important role between the continuing street markets of Petticoat Lane and Brick Lane, attracting young artists and designers. It is instrumental in the regeneration of the area.

Lamb Street, Spitalfields market, 1912.
(Courtesy of Tower Hamlets Local History Library & Archives)

Petticoat Lane

An important figure in the development of Hogge Lane was
Benedict Spinola (1520–1580), an Italian merchant who leased
ground there in the late 1500s.[2] He developed cottage housing for
the poor and larger houses for the rich, building up to 100 homes.
More and more foreign visitors were coming to London, but they
were frequently met with resistance and, indeed, riots; Hogge Lane
soon became a very popular place to trade, becoming a refuge for
many who took the opportunity, often out of necessity, to develop
an occupation in trade. Moreover, in around 1606 the Common
Council passed an Act in response to the great number of foreign
street hawkers that said: 'That no foreigner whatsoever should
presume to vend his, her or their goods in the city, by connivance
or otherwise, either in shop, house, stall or street upon the penalty
of £5 for every offence except such as brought provisions to the city.'
The huge fine had the desired effect and drove the hawkers, who sold
mostly second-hand clothes, out of the city and into Hogge Lane,
which was soon renamed Petticoat Lane, appearing for the first time
as such on Ryther's early seventeenth-century map of London.

At around the same time a further reference to the new name
occurs in Ben Jonson's play *The Devil is an Ass* (1616):

> Like a needle of Spain, with a thread at my tail
> We will survey the suburbs and make forth our sallies,
> Down Petticoat Lane and up the smock alleys,
> To Shoreditch, Whitechapel and so to St. Kathern's,
> To drink with the Dutch there, and take forth their patterns.

(Act 1, Scene 1)

2   A confession of this Italian trader marks an early example of traders' relationship
    with legalities and authority: in 1561, he admitted to exporting another trader's
    goods on his own licence but, remarkably, was allowed to maintain trading and
    continued to be an important person not only in the development of Hogge
    Lane but in other commerce and government affairs.

At this time in the seventeenth century Petticoat Lane was a desirable area, according to the ecclesiastical historian John Strype,
the son of John Strype (or van Strijp), who had come to London
to learn the business of silk 'throwster' from his uncle Abraham
van Strijp, of Dutch nationality, who, to escape religious persecution, had taken refuge in England. He, like many early settlers,
was Jewish. Strype later set up business for himself in what was
later known as Strypes Yard – now Strype Street – which forms
part of the Petticoat Lane market that still operates to this day.

Strype's references to 'Petticoat Lane' suggest a place where
some gentleman of the court and city had their town houses.
The most notable of these was the Spanish ambassador Hans
Jacobson, jeweller to King James I. However, the gentrification of
the area did not last long. In 1665 the bubonic plague struck and
in the following year the Great Fire of London devastated the city.
The map of London was about to be redrawn. New areas were
sought for settlement and business opportunities, and cheaper
housing became available. As a consequence of the rebuilding
of the city Petticoat Lane became populated by impoverished
workmen who needed to live close by their work, and so very
crowded streets of small houses were built in the area. The increase
of population necessitated the development of new street markets.
Furthermore, an Act of Parliament of 1674 banned street markets
within the city walls and, within a short time, Petticoat Lane became
the most sought-after area for further development in market
trading. The market, which developed to serve a growing number
of immigrants and the existing poor, affected the social standing of
the area and houses once populated by the rich were taken over by
businessmen and immigrants who began to trade there.

As noted earlier, the area then received a significant immigrant
influx of approximately 13,500 French Protestants fleeing from
religious persecution following the revocation of the Edict of
Nantes in 1685. A great number of these immigrants were silk
weavers who were extremely skilled at their work, but even with
these new skilled workers Strype still implies that the area had

lost its social standing. As discussed previously, the arrival of the French Huguenots was crucial to the development of the fabric in the area and in particular to Petticoat Lane. It is with these changes that, by the next century, the shape of Petticoat Lane market as we know it today had truly come into being.

Ghetto in the 'Lane'

The Lane was always the great marketplace, and every insalubrious street and alley abutting on it was covered with the overflowing of its commerce and its mud. Wentworth Street and Goulston Street were the chief branches, and in festival times the latter was a pandemonium of caged poultry, clucking and quacking and cackling and screaming. Fowls and geese and ducks were bought alive, and taken to have their throats cut for a fee by the official slaughterer. At Purim a gaiety, as of the Roman carnival, enlivened the swampy Wentworth Street, and brought a smile onto the unwashed face of the pavement.

Especially was this so at Passover, when for a week the poorest Jew must use a supplementary set of crockery and kitchen utensils. A babel of sound, audible for several streets around, denoted Market Day in Petticoat Lane, and the pavements were blocked by serried crowds going both ways at once. (Zangwill 1892)

During the 1700s the area was extremely shabby but well known as a district that anybody who had anything to sell would visit for that purpose. Jewish peasants from central Eastern Europe began to settle in the area, but found it extremely difficult to find employment because of their curious looks, their unusual religious practices – with Sabbath hours and holy days conflicting with those of the indigenous population – and, of course, the language barrier. The Jewish immigrants' salvation was thus Petticoat Lane market, where they sold whatever they could, almost inevitably second-hand clothes, to make ends meet. They carried out their sales partly in Yiddish and partly in cockney, slowly integrating into life on the market. Women found such occupation a particularly useful opportunity to earn a wage supplementing the family income.

The deterioration in the status of the area seems to have continued and was marked by levels of crime and disorder. For example, in 1747 the *General Evening News* reported that the master of the 'Cock Alehouse' in Petticoat Lane was tried at the Guildhall for keeping a disorderly house. Prostitution and the 'fencing' of stolen goods in public houses around the

Life in Petticoat Lane. (Courtesy of Bishopsgate Institute)

Life in London.   *After the black & white drawing by Clement Flower.*
Sunday Morning in Petticoat Lane.

Petticoat Lane on a Sunday morning. (Courtesy of Bishopsgate Institute)

market were commonplace. Other newspaper reports from the time refer to 'gangs of robbers keeping the inhabitants in continual fear'. One such report, from 1775, reported that 'There is a gang of robbers about Petticoat Lane and its vicinity not much less daring than the Black boy-alley gang, of infamous memory, who keep the inhabitants in continual dread.' Another report refers to 'Martha Cutler, Sarah Cowden and Sarah Storer for feloniously assaulting Henry Soloman in the dwelling house of Aaron Davis in Petticoat Lane, Dilings in Gun Court, Petticoat Lane and robbing him of £15 4s in money'. In 1787 the situation was so bad that the parish of Whitechapel had to appoint day and night patrols in the Lane and surrounding areas to protect its population.

The market continued to flourish in spite of – or perhaps because of – the poverty and degradation in the area. Although the Huguenot silk weaving trade was to enter a terminal decline with the Anglo-French free trade treaty of 1860, which allowed for the import of cheap French silk, the area was to develop in other ways. The Jewish refugees took advantage of the Huguenot houses as their dwellings and found their large windows eminently suitable for tailoring. Jewish and other immigrants also developed other craft and manufacturing trades, such as furniture making, but the markets of Petticoat Lane and Brick Lane ensured, in the flourishing of street trading, occupations for the many that did not possess such lucrative skills.

Exodus empire

The course of the nineteenth century saw a further enormous rise in the immigrant population, with many more Russian and East European Jews fleeing persecution, alongside Irish immigrants escaping the potato famine. Many of these immigrants settled in the East End and the 'Lanes' provided both a means of gaining an income and strong community bonds.

The area had a large Jewish population and the market has been associated with Jews from its inception. Because of the Sabbath, Sunday eventually became the main market trading day. The area was, as noted, extremely deprived and new immigrants who were half starving were helped by wealthy West End Jews, who set up various institutions to help its population, including soup kitchens and the Jewish Free School. Established in 1820, the Jewish Free School was originally built to house 900 pupils, but by 1907 had become the largest elementary school in the world, with more than 3,500 pupils. Alumni include the entertainer Bud Flanagan OBE and the diamond millionaire Barney Barnato. The Jewish Board of Guardians was also established. These organisations made a significant difference to the lives of many Jewish immigrants.

Aside from Jewish organisations, other philanthropists and organisations mobilised in the East End to help the poor and destitute. William Booth's Salvation Army developed from his Christian Revival Society, which was set up in 1865. Booth, who abandoned the Church for preaching the gospel on the streets, sought to 'rescue' drug addicts, alcoholics, prostitutes and the homeless through religious conversion and membership of his Christian army.

Despite these private philanthropic efforts, however, Petticoat Lane was a matter of deep concern to the authorities, its somewhat infamous reputation being seen as problematic. In an effort to try and get rid of the market they changed the street's name from Petticoat Lane to Middlesex Street (the street was at that time in the County of Middlesex) in 1830. This was also seen as a way of excising an embarrassing reference to a female undergarment. The new name was ignored by the East End inhabitants, however, who continued to refer to the market as Petticoat Lane. Much to the dissatisfaction of the authorities the market, far from disappearing with the name change, continued to expand and grew yet more popular.

Petticoat Lane was an area of shops and street traders. Half of all shops by 1850 sold new or second-hand clothing. Henry Mayhew, in his book *London Labour and the London Poor*, wrote:

Embracing the streets and adjacent to Petticoat Lane and including rows of old boots on the ground there is between two and three miles of old clothes. Petticoat Lane proper is long and narrow and to look down it is to look down a vista of many coloured garments. These things, mixed with the hues of the women's garments, spotted and stripped [sic] certainly present a scheme which cannot be beheld in any other part of the greatest city in the world, nor in any other portion of the world itself.

Another valuable insight into Petticoat Lane in the mid-1800s is contained in Watts Philips' book *The Wild Tribes of London*. He relates the familiar accounts of criminal activity, notably the 'fencing' of stolen goods, and notes that, in the Lane, one is 'surrounded by thieves on all sides'. Although, of course, these reports add to the market's disreputable image, in another passage he describes the market in extraordinary terms, conjuring up a place that must have filled and intoxicated the senses:

Here, also are merchants from Smyrna and Constantinople, dealers from Hamburgh, Frankfort and a host of towns beside; two Russian Jews from Siberia and one shrivelled little monkey-faced Hebrew from Morrocco. They are speaking languages of all kinds … And we look upon men who have travelled from all corners of the earth to trade and to trade in Petticoat Lane.

Petticoat Lane's reputation, despite its importance to and popularity among the local community, continued to be derided in the press. For example, in *The City Press* of 20 August 1881 an article describes:

… the market [as] one of the curiosities of London. As a lively and literal picture of low life it is not to be surpassed and for students of certain phases of metropolitan existence it possesses a peculiar fascination … The sellers in expatiating on the value of their goods, employ figures of speech which are apt to jar upon polite ears …

From end to end the street is packed with [a] noisy, sweltering
mob, Jew and gentile herding together indiscriminately, and the
distinctions of race seeming to blend in a mass of uniform ugliness.

The Lane would receive further notoriety on 30 September 1888,
when Catherine Eddowes was killed in Mitre Square, a short
distance from Petticoat Lane. Her garments were torn and a part
of them was found in Goulston Street (an area of Petticoat Lane
market); on the wall above was graffiti: 'The Juwes are not the men
that will be blamed for nothing.' This incident has since become
part of the Jack the Ripper mythology and theories abound regarding
its meaning, but there can be no mistaking that the message linked
the murders to the local Jewish community. It is not known whether
the blame attaches to a person from another community who used
the Jews as a scapegoat or whether the culprit was of Jewish origin
but, of course, the murder only cemented the view that the area,
including the market, was nothing more than a den of iniquity.

Alongside the market's reputation as a place of thieves, shabbi-
ness and unholy alliances was a stereotypical perception on the
part of the public of Jews as scrooges and swindlers. It was clear,
though, that the Jewish community was at pains to assimilate
and be accepted into British society, despite a growing tide of
discrimination. Although the market was a place of lawlessness
it remained an intrinsic part of the immigrant community simply
because poverty was the great leveller and the market provided
the means and mechanisms to navigate survival.

An example of the importance of the market to immigrant
communities was Leyden Street, where there are now decaying
and boarded-up Victorian toilets. It was once the area where
the Jewish community would debate politics and current events,
and was widely known as the Parliament of Petticoat Lane.
Leyden Street is not the street it was and I recall that, only a few
years ago, when the toilets were open to the public, it was plagued
by anti-social behaviour, drug use, prostitution and 'cottaging'.
In fact, for a short time market officers were instructed to patrol

and root out any disreputable behaviour. This was a task dreaded by the officers but made slightly more amusing by one of the elder Jewish female traders on the market, Karen Goldman, who would bellow down into the toilet basement 'Cocks in, trousers up!' Leyden Street is now undergoing refurbishment, and smart new apartments are being built around the site.

In the areas surrounding the market people of various ethnicities tended to live in their own community 'pockets', in particular the Irish community, who lived in and around the notorious Dorset Street, the poorest street of London, renowned for being 'the worst street in London'. Russian and East European Jews lived in their own hierarchical communities in other areas surrounding Petticoat Lane. In attempting to overcome the many distressing problems of crime and poverty, the various immigrant communities looked to the market of Petticoat Lane for a chance to progress from abject poverty and deprivation. Different nationalities traded side-by-side in an enduring struggle for subsistence in the biggest open market sprawl in the world.

Sunday market, Petticoat Lane, c.1890. (Courtesy of Bishopsgate Institute)

A typical scene in Petticoat Lane, *c*.1910. (Courtesy of Bishopsgate Institute)

The particular themes of poverty, crime and politics, and the market's growth into the twentieth century, I shall explore in more detail below. It was clear, however, that at the end of the nineteenth century Petticoat Lane was destined to play a significant part in London's development and, in particular, in the expansion of population and economic growth in the East End.

Lawlessness and poverty

The growth of Petticoat Lane was a cause for grave concern in Victorian society. This lawless area, populated by immigrants, was ostensibly out of control. The authorities had tried unsuccessfully to manage the area: newspaper reports show that from the middle of the 1800s the police tried to put an end to the 'Petticoat Lane nuisance', after many complaints had been made. However, this had little effect on the Jewish traders, who 'continued their business within the mart as usual'.

The Petticoat Lane market can be imagined as a lifebelt for the drowning poor, as a place where there was a chance to make a living and to avoid succumbing to prostitution and homelessness. The marketplace became a great cultural leveller, with all plying for trade side by side. The traders of Petticoat Lane were an unusual, strong and independent force bonded by poverty – but, as a haven for the poor, the market was also attractive to the dark criminal underbelly of London.

The Jewish immigrant in particular gained a reputation for criminality and undesirable activity. There were many reasons for this perception, which was not always unjustified. But, as the website Moving Here (www.movinghere.org.uk) suggests, 'Jews were more or less forced to cluster in insecure occupations where there was a narrow borderline between straight and improper practice'. The Jewish population were forced to live by their wits, as were the other immigrant communities, as they were often excluded from more respectable jobs. It is no wonder that various criminal and underworld practices were adopted as means of survival. The marketplace could thus be not only the buffer zone between an immigrant and abject poverty but also an arena of undesirable activity.

As early as the mid-1800s, Petticoat Lane's notoriety came to the attention of Parliament, and, in an extensive article published in *The Builder* of 3 July 1858, the area comes under close scrutiny. In describing the Jewish trading and the market's great size it stated: '… it has been shown that vast numbers of persons congregate here every Sunday morning, partly to traffic and partly for plunder.' Citing the lord mayor's concern, the writer questioned whether the 'evil could not be abated'. A noteworthy comment is made regarding a problem that has never been fully addressed: that Middlesex Street fell, and indeed still falls, under two different jurisdictions, the City of London and the local authority of Tower Hamlets, as it is now. Although the article's tone is a negative one, it does finally suggest, on a more conciliatory note, that the market serves a purpose and is in need of a more thoughtful approach to its perceived problems:

> The scene is marvellous, and it might be useful if those who have the making of laws would visit such places, to glance at the vast thousands who are crushed together, and study the circumstances under which they are placed. There is something in the sight which suggests the necessity of sanitary measures.

In 1871 *The City Press* described the growing media concern:

> The lane is a vivid place dominated by the Sunday trading day where 'Jewish hawkers' dominate the market, selling old clothes. Every valueless item made to look worth something was sold, every female garment from heels, caps to Petticoats. The market was packed with Jews from every area of London numbering thousands … The buyers are so numerous that you do not venture to state how many; you only know that there is so dense a crowd that you can scarcely make your way through it.

The writer continues on the themes of 'lawlessness', race and immigration, describing the market as a breeding ground for crime: as many as 2,000 thieves who live in the 'alleys and surrounding area are drawn to the Sunday market like birds of prey … Everything which meets your eyes and ears is painful in the extreme and although many additional policeman are engaged, the place is rife with all tricks of unrighteousness.'

A decade later *The City Press* of August 1881, referring to a letter from a Mr Arthur Klein, describes in vivid detail the lawlessness in the market:

> An occasional drunken figure lends animation to the scene, and sometimes there is a rush among 'the uglies' to the rescue of a thief whom the police – doubled and trebled in numbers on Sunday – have detected in the exercise of his calling. From end to end the street is packed with a noisy, sweltering mob, Jew and Gentile herding together indiscriminately, and the distinctions of race seeming to blend together in a mass uniform of ugliness.

The market was, according to this writer, home to extensive thieving and probable trade in stolen and obscene goods, as well as being a place where dangerous persons dwelt. Scorn is poured on the name-change from Petticoat Lane to Middlesex Street as 'a well meant but almost childish effort … to purchase respectability for the place'. The writer quotes Mr Klein as describing the market as '"the great capital of thiefdom, and the training college whence the younger go forth to prey upon society"', and finishes in dramatic fashion: Petticoat Lane 'is an ugly blot upon the map of the city and we commend it to the attention of the Commissioners of Sewers'. In the following year *The City Press* reported early attempts by the authorities to control Petticoat Lane, in which orders were issued to discontinue the market:

> An order has been issued from the chief office of the Police, Old Jewry, that this gathering was to be discontinued, but upon representations that it has been in existence for 200 years, and that help would be given to do away with some of its worst features the order was withdrawn but some of its more objectionable accompaniments will be abolished henceforth.

The market was also reluctantly seen in some quarters as a fundamental part of London life, if only as a bizarre curiosity to be enjoyed by the Jewish immigrant, as reported in *The Quiver*, a Christian journal, in the late 1800s: 'the Jew, for instance, has had his Sabbath and now the Christian Sunday has arrived he comes forth to enjoy himself in his own way.' The growing anti-Semitic sentiment of the day is evident here in the deriding of the Jewish identity, the writer describing in stereotypical racist language the Jewish individual's great 'capacity for laziness and holiday making'. This is seen too in another article from the same journal, in which the Young Men's Christian Association meeting was reported: their concern over Petticoat Lane market reveals perhaps more anti-Jewish sentiment than anxiety over the area's 'lawlessness'. One speaker is quoted as bemoaning the

Sunday market as a demise of Christian values: '[It] was a terrible commentary on our boasted civilization and Christianity.'

The Sunday trading on Petticoat Lane certainly concerned the Christian authorities, as it challenged their morality and traditions. An article from 1871 describes Petticoat Lane on Sunday: 'There is not a particle of Sabbath about it and you do not feel it to be Sunday until you are beyond the reach of its din and bustle, its haggling and profane atmosphere.' However, not all contemporary writers took the same view. A rare but welcome report from *The Illustrated News* of 15 April 1893 entitled 'Passover eve in Petticoat Lane – the merrymaking of Israel in London' describes the rich traditions and joys of the festivities in the market – its many costumes, foodstuffs and people: 'it is a strange and wonderful crowd of a strange and wonderful people.'

The unruliness of both Petticoat Lane and, indeed, Brick Lane markets should be set against the well-documented backdrop of extreme poverty and hardship in these areas. Charles Booth's *Descriptive Map of East End Poverty*, made in the late 1800s, documents the East End as the poorest part of London, although a few years later he suggested that parts of south London were worse. Interestingly and most crucially, he also indicates the important role of markets in a developing London:

> The itinerant vendor plays a part in the life of London which has no parallel in any other city with which I am acquainted; and of his class the costermonger or street-seller of perishable goods is the most important. His role is to save his customers the trouble of going to market by taking the market to them and in connection with the facilities thus offered and as natural result of the growth of London the original retail markets have assumed an almost wholesale character. From these markets the retail shops obtain their supplies and to them the costermonger repairs to replenish his stock.

The Industrial Revolution, while bringing wealth to some, also brought squalor and poverty to the East End. With new factories opening, a hierarchy quickly developed among the various trades and occupations. The descendants of the Huguenot immigrants tended to be employed in skilled labour, while the market trader was much lower down the pecking order – but not as low as some, as Ed Glinert describes in his excellent book *East End Chronicles*: 'the market trader … knew he was socially superior to a full-time employee such as the pure picker who made a living collecting dog turds dropped in the streets'.

Such was the hardship of life on the market that it is no surprise that any means possible to achieve subsistence was employed, including, by some, petty crime, as is well observed in Watts Philips' book *The Wild Tribes of London* (1855). Here he describes dealing in stolen goods:

> These men are known to the initiated as Petticoat-lane fencers, or receivers of stolen goods. Patiently they sit in these filthy rooms, waiting news from their scouts, who they throw out as antennae to 'feel the way'; or for the appearance of the thief's confederate, who 'gives the office', and tells where the booty may be found. The Jew asks no questions, makes his 'pargain', and in a few hours the articles themselves have ceased to exist – or, rather, have been born again in a form that their original fashioner would refuse to own them.

This was a fight for survival and the marketplace was its amphitheatre.

It was during the Victorian period that the term costermonger became particularly prevalent. It dates back certainly to the sixteenth century and possibly to the thirteenth century (coster is a corruption of costard, a kind of apple), but in the nineteenth century it was applied to the many street hawkers who sold fruit – or other food items, such as hot eels, whelks and potatoes – on the street, which they obtained directly from wholesalers. The hawkers and costermongers were very often the poorest in Victorian society and sought desperately to make a living. One of the most lucid and informative first-hand accounts of life in the East End is contained in Jack London's book *The People of the Abyss*:

The costers wheel loads of specked and decaying fruit around in the barrows all day, and very often store it in their one living and sleeping room for the night. There it is exposed to the sickness and disease, the effluvia and vile exhalations of overcrowded and rotten life, and next day it is carted.

The rich culture developed by the costers is evident in many aspects of life, such as language and dress. Particularly interesting is the development of cockney back slang, a secret language used to confuse the authorities and laypeople alike; the term 'esclop' meant 'police', for example. In addition, the most successful costermongers developed a very distinctive style of dress – perhaps after that of Henry Croft, a street sweeper famed for his charitable work in the East End – decorated with mother-of-pearl buttons, which were manufactured in East End factories. Those wearing this wardrobe were called Pearly Kings and Queens, and were considered in high standing among the costermonger community. Pearly Kings and Queens spent a considerable amount of time collecting money for charity and to this day can still be seen on the markets of Petticoat Lane and Brick Lane.

Buying chickens in Wentworth Street, *c*.1910.
(Courtesy of Tower Hamlets Local History Library & Archives)

Wentworth Street, Petticoat Lane, c.1905.
(Courtesy of Tower Hamlets Local History Library & Archives)

However, the costers were not to everyone's liking and, apart
from exasperating the authorities they infuriated shopkeepers,
who saw costers trading without paying rent and poaching their
customers. The first step of legitimacy for the street trader/hawker
or costermonger came in 1894, when the Court of Appeal allowed
the continuation of the costermongers' business free from local
authority interference as long as they complied with price regulations. In effect, this ruling legitimised the street market and,
in particular, the trading of the costermonger, but also of other
street traders. Nonetheless, even with some newfound legitimacy,
the lawlessness was far from over.

With Petticoat Lane thus in its ascendancy at the turn of the
century the market was again depicted in a predominantly adverse
light by much of the contemporary press. This did little to temper
Petticoat Lane's popularity, however; at this time it was a thriving
street market with a myriad of street traders offering an assortment
of clothes, tools and food, as well as hawkers selling racing tips.
The Lane was so fashionable that traders fought each other for
pitches in a largely anarchic and lawless sprawl.

Old Castle Street, *c*.1905. (Courtesy of Bishopsgate Institute)

Social reform

From the late nineteenth century social campaigners began to demand improvements to the conditions of the poor. The impact of these changes would be immensely significant for both the communities of the East End and the markets' status. The trade union movement, socialism and the suffragette movement all have deep involvement in or connections with the East End.

Among the most significant campaigners was William Booth, a missionary Christian who dedicated much of his life to helping the poor of the East End. He set up the Christian Revival Society (later the Christian Mission) in 1865, from which developed, more famously, the Salvation Army. The strong Christian beliefs and moral compass of the Salvation Army had enormous benefits for many of the poor but it could be argued that the emphasis thus placed on the Christian holy day of Sunday was a hindrance to Petticoat Lane's fight for legal Sunday trading. A statue of William Booth was erected in his honour on the junction of Mile End Road and Whitechapel Road; slightly tarnished today, it is a stark reminder to me when travelling into work of the East End's squalid and destitute history and the social reformers who attempted to change the area – particularly on those occasions when, ironically, a homeless person is seen asleep at the base of the iconic statue.

Other significant reformers and organisations include Thomas John Barnardo, who set up the Ragged Schools for orphaned children in 1867 after the previous year's cholera epidemic, which was responsible for the deaths of more than 3,000 people in the East End. In 1884, in Commercial Street, practically opposite Petticoat Lane market, Toynbee Hall was set up by Samuel and Henrietta Barnett. This was the first settlement university of the settlement movement and was named in memory of Arnold Toynbee, fellow reformer and historian. The organisation sought to educate privileged university students in the reality of poverty and depravation first-hand, through their living in the East End slums.

Famous residents include Clement Attlee, William Beveridge and John Profumo. Toynbee Hall continues its work to this day in a number of charitable areas and was an inspiration for the development of the modern social worker.

The work carried out by Toynbee Hall seems quite enlightened, even by today's standards. Although Petticoat Lane and the surrounding area did suffer with high crime rates, gangs and prostitution, the social reformers realised that only by fully understanding the deprived areas through living and working in them could they make valid judgements about their communities. They recognised that the attitudes that tended to prevail among those of their own faith and class damned the lives of people in the area as a threat, nuisance and scourge upon society.

Developing improvement through true understanding of the issues was instrumental in creating a more just society. Yet it is disquieting that in some respects we appear to be turning the clock back in terms of challenging poverty and working-class stereotypes. How many are campaigning today in the way that earlier social reformers did? It could be said that in some ways the Victorian age was a more enlightened time, with a more caring intellectual elite who were set upon alleviating poverty and misery through improving the social conditions of the East End, rather than merely damning them.

The social reformer who perhaps had the most direct impact on Petticoat Lane and the market life of east London, however, was Angela Burdett-Coutts, a friend of Charles Dickens. Born in 1814, she became a philanthropist after inheriting over £2 million from her grandfather. She assisted in the setting up of a home for young women to help them turn away from a life of prostitution, and also gave support to the Ragged Schools, soup kitchens and housing schemes for the working classes, as well as campaigning for the prevention of cruelty to children. It was her work in developing a market in Columbia Road, however, that is most significant in terms of the markets and environment of the East End.

Despite the efforts of previous campaigners, however, poverty and 'social reform' continue to be a major concern, particularly in the borough of Tower Hamlets: alongside prostitution are other stark reminders of poverty that have not left the East End. Homelessness is rife, sleeping rough and begging are commonplace. In fact, on Wentworth Street, opposite the market, is a homeless shelter that feeds the needy on a daily basis. The borough's street markets, too, remain a contentious issue.

2

TOBYS, TRADERS AND THE MARKET

Nefarious streets

'The Abyss', 'The Ghetto' and 'slum' were all historical references to the area known as the East End, in particular the streets of Whitechapel, the area surrounding Spitalfields and the markets of Petticoat Lane and Brick Lane. This notorious district, with its dark legacy, retains the foreboding atmosphere that the area was famous for.

Retracing the steps I had first taken in the early 1990s, I recall my first impressions of the area. The locale surrounding the market, although smattered with clothes shops displaying the faded fashions of previous years, luggage emporiums and chicken shops, was brimming with notable historical landmarks. I was already aware of the outstanding Whitechapel art gallery and the burgeoning private galleries opening up in the area which was, prior to the contemporary Spitalfields development, immediately fascinating to me. As an aficionado of true crime history I was, of course, also aware of the Jack the Ripper legacy and the history of the Kray twins. The locality of Spitalfields and Brick Lane is now the most fashionable area in London and part of its charm is that it still evokes a great sense of the past, but back in the mid-1990s it felt as though the area was still frozen in time. The streets were yet to be discovered by guidebooks or filled with bars to cater for tourists; in essence, the Victorian past was within touching distance, resonating with the allure of its previous incarnation.

Hawksmoor's Christ Church, opposite Spitalfields market, is an exquisite sight and wholly dominates the area. It is, in my opinion, the most striking church in London. Built between 1714 and 1729 as one of a number of churches in the East End, it has been the place of worship for many waves of immigrants, though more recently has achieved a wider repute through Iain Sinclair's contention that the Hawksmoor churches formed a pattern consistent with Theistic Satanism. The gardens of the church, now cleared, are home to numerous vagrants, creating their own congregation of drunken oblivion. Further along is a nightclub housed in an abandoned public toilet, steps leading down from street level to underground revelry. The dazed and weary young clubbers reappear in the early hours of Sunday mornings, greeted only by passing market traders' vans and accompanied by the solitary wanderings of street prostitutes trying to entice a final punter.

Adjacent to Christ Church are some of the most remarkable period houses in London: the French Huguenot houses, of which those in Fournier Street and Princelet Street are fine examples. No. 19 Princelet Street, now an unrestored museum, is an exquisite place to encounter the lives of generations of immigrants to the area. Built in 1719, the house was initially home to a silk-weaving family and was later the dwelling of Jewish residents, who built a synagogue in its basement. It is an outstanding building that should be regarded with extreme pride as among London's finest museums.

As is typical of the area, with the smooth there is the rough – or, at least, the legacy of such. On the corner of Fournier Street and Commercial Street is the public house The Ten Bells, which was the pub where two of the Ripper's victims, Annie Chapman and Mary Kelly, were known to have been drinking before meeting their grim fate. Ironically, in the mid-1990s the pub was a strip-tease establishment: young women pole danced to a background of Ripper literature and pictures adorning the walls. To say this was distasteful is probably an understatement; nevertheless, it still held a fascination for me, as it showed such a direct link between present and past. The pub was even called the 'Jack the Ripper' from 1976 to 1988. However, it has reinvented itself again in the last couple of years, and the strippers and Ripper memorabilia have been replaced by comfortable sofas and romantic lighting: it is now a beacon for voguish tourists and fashionistas.

Petticoat Lane contains a great legacy of the area, and yet when I first encountered it its history remained elusive to me. Nonetheless, it was still plainly the epicentre of life, the heart of the East End, and its tales began to fascinate and seduce me.

A strange new world

Eighteen years ago, in 1996, I gained employment with Tower Hamlets Council as a part-time market inspector. I was thrown in at the deep end: my first day's duty was a Sunday, the busiest trading day. Little did I realise what a disorientating, disturbing and exhilarating experience it would be.

Our offices, based in Commercial Street under Denning Point tower block – soon to be demolished to give way to a shopping development – were, at that time at the height of the markets' success, a hive of activity. From seven o'clock in the morning bedraggled and anxious market traders gathered outside our office, peering in through the grated window, hoping to catch the eye of an inspector and encourage him to open up the office so that they could be allocated a pitch for the day. The numbers grew by the minute, but the increasing noise, thuds on the window and meaningful glances did little to persuade the market team to open the doors. The traders were made to wait until a designated time, once all preparations were completed, cups of tea drunk and stories of the previous Saturday night exchanged. If I thought at the time that this attitude seemed laissez-faire, however, I was mistaken.

When the doors were finally opened frenzied activity began. Market inspectors took positions at four separate desks guarded by protective glass and began the process of collecting the licence cards and vouchers from probably well over 100 casual traders. Licences were allocated in such a way that the longest-serving traders were at the top of the priority list, but that, needless to say, was far from the end of the process. According to other rules and regulations, traders selling the same commodity could not work next to one another and even a seemingly discrete commodity such as ladies' wear was sub-divided into several more: blouses, trousers and jackets, for example. The positions of traders' pitches was also supposed to be rotated so that they did not expect or demand a certain pitch, although this injunction, of course, ran contrary to the priority system and was later slowly dropped.

Pitch allocation was not, therefore, a straightforward process, but rather a jostling campaign for the best pitches, with traders arguing among themselves and pleading with the inspector, citing previous transgressions and poor conduct on the part of their rivals in support of their own applications. Long-standing traders would try as though their lives depended on it to convince the inspectors that they must secure their desired pitch. Eventually, however, the pitches were allocated by the inspectors in a seemingly fair and proper manner, the traders slowly cleared away from the office to the market and the inspectors had the time to breathe a sigh of relief that the first important task of the day was completed.

It was clear to me from that short introduction that the job was going to take some nerve, strength of character and determination to deal with the complexities of the traders, and possibly also the inspectors', forcefulness and volatility, and as yet I had not even stepped out into the market.

When I did, walking out into Wentworth Street – the heart of Petticoat Lane market – with the other inspectors, we were soon faced with a myriad of apparently chaotic and angry traders, who were quarrelling again about pitches: new traders had just arrived at the market and set up on pitches not allocated to them. Some were in tears, others shouting, and it seemed that a few were on the brink of attacking their rivals. Vans were moving in and out of the market, horns were sounding and goods were being unloaded. In between was the odd visitor or tourist, who had made the mistake of arriving too early and found themselves in a version of Dante's hell.

As far as I was concerned this certainly qualified as being 'thrown into the deep end'. I was hauled into the battleground that was Petticoat Lane, separating the combatants, sorting out pitch issues and attempting to impose some semblance of order and peace, which was finally achieved with a combination of persuasion and threats. The reporting of a trader for breaching their licence conditions was my legal tool under the London Local Authorities Act; prosecution could follow. I quite quickly came to the conclusion that without this tool we would be a toothless power, but it also became apparent that, more than this, I would have to gain the trust and respect of the traders if I was to be capable of doing the job in the way that was required.

Gaining the trust of the traders would prove to be more than a morning's work. On the market I was first introduced to a tall, well-built Asian trader with gangling arms and a slightly menacing look in his eyes. The trader, who seemed intrigued by my appearance, mumbled – almost unintelligibly – 'Who's the new Toby then?' And then he proceeded to punch me in the stomach. It wasn't intended to hurt me but the shock sent me stumbling backwards, to shouts of laughter from traders and inspectors alike. Once I'd regained my composure I introduced myself to the trader, saying that I was pleased to meet him, and told him never to repeat his introduction again in the most robust terms I could muster.

The origins of the Toby

That was the first time that I had heard the term 'Toby', a slang name given to inspectors. The founding of the role of market inspector went back to 1927, when under the General Powers Act Stepney Council took over the running of the street markets as they sought to exert control over the state of lawlessness that surrounded them. There are only a few historical references to the term 'Toby', but A *Dictionary of Slang and Unconventional English* (Partridge and Beale 2002) refers to the 'Tober-mush', a market inspector in Petticoat Lane. The early connotation of the word 'tober' appears to mean someone who will trick or rob you, and the word seems to have developed via a cockney rhyming slang word 'Toby Jug' (meaning a mug/fool). Hence 'who's the new Toby' is a warning word from the trader, employing a generally derogatory term for the inspector.

There is some ambiguity over this term, however, which seems in some quarters to refer to either the inspector or the market rig operator, as is suggested in the glossary of the website for Gavin Kenning engineering (www.market-stalls.co.uk), in which 'toby' is defined as the rent for a pitch on site, while 'Toby man' is the person who collects the rent. Frena Bloomfields, in an article entitled 'Nothing is for Nothing' in the *Guardian* on 16 January 1970, notes: 'There's Sammy in orange socks standing on a stall, nails between his teeth, cursing as he tries to hammer his rickety stalls together. Sammy is a Toby man – he lets out stalls at ten bob a week.' Bloomfields goes on to describe a conspiratorial deal going on between Sammy the Toby man and illegal street traders/hawkers for a prime pitch that they can stake a claim to until the inspector arrives to licence the pitches. This was obviously before the days of a more formally regulated market. Indeed, Bloomfields refers to an eccentric character named Solly who notes, of the good old days, 'there were no licensed stallholders and traders used to fight sometimes to the death for a chance of a stall'.

Her article continues with a less than flattering description
of the market inspector, in which fly-pitchers have spotted the
inspectors, scrambled up their possessions and fled to nearby
side streets:

> There they are, three of them walking like kings down the centre of the
> street. Whatever they are in the scale of local government here they
> are the kings. And they have their own court, a little band of followers
> patting their backs, laughing immoderately at their jokes and generally
> fawning around. And why not: it can make the difference between
> ninety quid and nothing at all on whether or not they give you a stall
> for the day … If you can catch their eyes you're half way there. If you
> mutter the stall you want without any of the other boys hearing you
> you're home. So we get our stall. Quite right too. We've spent a year
> building up contacts with these moody overlords, dropping a note here
> and there and it's nice to see them bringing back dividends.

This occupation, then, was one with a long and ambiguous
backstory; there were also rumours of freemasonry being linked
to past generations of inspectors. Although it was yet to fully dawn
on me what I had let myself in for, it quickly appealed to me as
a fascinating job where there would be little time to get bored,
as Petticoat Lane was clearly a thriving market and a prominent
feature of east London street life.

The impact of the Tobys

In 1965 the County of Middlesex was abolished and the London
Borough of Tower Hamlets was formed from the former metropolitan boroughs of Bethnal Green, Poplar and Stepney. The new
governing bodies immediately sought to take more control of the
markets. The deployment of new market inspectors would have a
stabilising effect on the market, combating lawlessness and slowly
introducing fair systems for the allocation of pitches. The new

authority also sought to deal with disorder, minor infringements and illegal trading, as well as the sub-letting of pitches, which, however, was to be a serious problem for the market and the authority for years to come.

The inspector's main tasks were to licence temporary traders, resolve disputes and ensure a safe and legal market: to generally be the 'police' officer of the market. In the armoury of the inspector, as noted previously, was and is the power to report traders and illegal traders with the view for the council to prosecute offenders and or revoke licences of persistent offenders. The market is now governed under the London Local Authorities Act 1990 (as amended). The legislation relating to the market consists of a long list of rules and regulations by which the trader must abide. There are rules about correct pitch size, selling only the commodities that one has been licensed for, trading in person, from the correct pitch and within prescribed hours, and so on. The list is a long one and the trader's responsibilities are thus many and varied. These conditions under the Act can be amended as needed but changes must be committee approved. The importance of the Act lies in the fact that it helps to protect the public (consumers) and traders alike, as well as being a tool for the council to enforce breaches of conditions as necessary.

The heavy burden of rules was perhaps necessary to regulate the market at first, particularly in light of the post-war boom, but by the time I started on the market some regulations were starting to look somewhat draconian and unyielding. They were challenging for the inspector to enforce and frustrating for the trader to adhere to. Although it is absolutely necessary to have a sensible legislative framework it also became necessary to adapt to, respond to and update the conditions of the market as circumstances dictated. The system is now far more receptive to traders' needs as well as offering protection to the public, but the demand to keep the market efficient, safe and productive is always a challenging one that is always under review.

A review of historic documented cases of prosecutions against traders reveals that some of the offences, as well as the arguments made in court, were quite extraordinary, while an examination of London Borough Committee market reports dating back to the 1960s throws up some interesting statistical data surrounding the policing of the market. The reports cover offences committed by traders and the inspectors who reported the traders, who at that time worked under the London County Council (General Powers) Act 1947.

One particular case that reached committee hearings to decide a trader's suitability to hold a licence following a prosecution and court action was for an unlawful act of standing on a box to attract trade. A background report in 1966 detailing events from two years previously states that the former Stepney Council took exception at stallholders standing on boxes or stalls as it caused large crowds to congregate around those stalls and impinged on the trade of other licensees. The practice by a certain number of stallholders had led to a number of complaints from other licensees, and the market inspectors were therefore instructed to submit details of all traders who conducted their trade by standing on their stalls. Twenty-six traders were 'reported', including eight who had previously given an undertaking to cease this practice.

The report goes on to say that out of the 1,400 traders working on a Sunday the practice was followed by a comparatively small handful of traders and although there was no specific bye-law which prohibited standing on stalls the action was seen as misconduct and therefore action under the General Powers Act should be pursued against the traders. It appears that all licensees heeded the warning apart from a Mr Cohen who continued the practice, prompting further committee reports.

In 1966 action was taken against Mr Cohen for trading above 'ground level'. The solicitor's arguments and the committee report are quite detailed: the case for the prosecution cites other traders' complaints about Mr Cohen's use of the practice and the fact that other traders had been warned off the practice and had ceased their behaviour. Mr Cohen had ignored those warnings and continued to be seen to take advantage over other traders. If the council were to ignore Mr Cohen's ongoing infringement it would weaken their authority and 'other traders would not be slow to take advantage again'.

Mr Cohen defended his actions thus: he was a man of short stature who was unable to sell from ground level. The unique position of his stall prohibited a level playing field with other stalls and he believed that no other street trader had complained about his practice. Finally, though, Mr Cohen conceded the position to the council to save his licence from being revoked and agreed to cease standing on a box to 'elevate' his trade.

Another example of a case that went to committee hearing, this time in 1972, is that of a trader, Mrs Singer, who had been reported for selling T-shirts alongside jumpers. At that time traders had very specific licences to sell a particular commodity group. For example, ladies' clothes were split into three different commodities (tops and jumpers; skirts and trousers; and undergarments) and never could a trader mix the commodities. At the time competition was fierce on the market and traders with the same commodity had to be at least three pitches apart. Because of the court action against Mrs Singer for selling an 'incorrect' clothes item the case went before the committee for possible revocation of licence. The report is detailed in its attempts to define T-shirts as different from tops and clearly finds the definition awkward, as 'of course garments which used to be worn by one sex are now being worn by both', even going as far as to refer to *Webster's Dictionary* for an answer. The situation was resolved and although T-shirts were defined as being different from tops, a compromise was reached and the case was finally dismissed. Thankfully the system has now been modified.

Mr Cohen's and Mrs Singer's cases are the tip of the iceberg. Many traders were reported for various offences on the market, and it is easy with hindsight to ridicule the seemingly petty nature of the offences outlined (although there were certainly more serious offences committed, such as illegal trading, sub-letting of pitches and mock auctions). However, until the early 1990s it was a difficult task to keep some semblance of order and fairness in the market, given its sheer scale and the enormous number of traders. A fine balancing act was needed on the part of the market inspector to keep a check on the market without being overbearing, and from the point of view of the trader such cases certainly highlight the depth of pettiness and jealousies that must have existed between stallholders, as well as their relationships with authority. It could be said, perhaps, that the rules should have been reviewed more frequently and their relevance properly confirmed.

The Toby men

My fellow Tobys were a curious hotchpotch of personalities in a very much male-dominated workforce; of a team of approximately twenty inspectors, only two were female. At that time the job required boldness and bluster and, as a result, attracted slightly eccentric and robust characters. One female colleague was an ex-prison warden and another an ex-traffic warden. In fact, most of the market officers had some kind of enforcement background; I and three or four other officers had parking enforcement backgrounds, another was a TV licensing man and others had a military background. It was not only the market traders, therefore, who had some unusual eccentricities: several of my colleagues also stood out in this way. I can only assume that in the extraordinary and dynamic world of the market the inspectors had to be of equal measure.

However, nothing had quite prepared me for one or two of the personalities that I was now introduced to and working alongside. A lot of the inspectors had nicknames that hinted at particular traits. For example, one inspector had a nasty habit of creeping up on market traders and catching them out for late trading, booking as many as he could. As it turned out, he was also vindictive towards some of his colleagues. Soon after I started on the job he suggested that we needed to take a trip to Ilford to pick up some office equipment. I thought at the time that this was a little unusual, particularly on a busy Sunday morning, but I reasoned that I was in an unusual job. Thus we travelled to Ilford, some 15 miles away, in the inspector's car, and duly parked outside an office supply shop – which was, unsurprisingly, closed. He merely commented that this was a shame and started the journey back to work, but, just outside Ilford, he quickly pointed at a row of 1930s terraced houses and claimed that he'd seen a colleague outside his home who should have been on duty in the market. I looked over and saw nobody at all. Although this seemed odd, it did not prepare me for the aftermath of this ruse. Coming back to work on the Tuesday, after a day off, I was questioned by my supervisor: 'So you saw an inspector on Sunday outside his house? Your colleague says you both saw him when he should have been working. He's in a lot of trouble.' Absolutely amazed, I said in no uncertain terms that I hadn't seen anyone – that, in fact, I hadn't witnessed anything at all. I went on to tell the whole story, while my supervisor just shook his head in bewilderment. Unbeknown to me at the time, he had a long history with the other inspector and was constantly trying to get him into trouble! After his dismissal it was rumoured that his response was a letter to the head of department threatening to 'crush his balls'. This did cause some amusement among the team but we were all glad to be rid of him. And, for me, it was an important lesson: to wise up.

As the older inspectors left they were replaced by new blood held up to more rigorous modern standards of recruitment, in which more quantifiable proof of experience and education was demanded. The expectations had developed, but this did not necessarily mean that new recruits were always of superior stature, however, and, as often was the case with market officers, there seem to have been a large number of maverick personalities attracted to the job. The new recruits, while invariably retaining a high level of professionalism, had some of these traits, some being more productive than others. One officer with a police background was nicknamed 'Hawkeye' for his ability to spot illegal activity within the market area from almost any distance. He formed part of a specialist team within markets dealing with illegal trading and was much praised for the work he carried out. Two other intelligent officers with creative flare and a passion for the markets' survival worked during their own time on a remodelled design for Whitechapel market. Their ideas became part of the springboard for the Olympic investment project 'High Street 2012'.

I was among the new recruits who strove to achieve the new professional standard of duties and conduct in the market. Another was Rob, one of the most gentle-natured men I have ever known. He was extremely well read, and had somehow found his way into the market job having previously been a TV licensing officer – thus fulfilling the obligatory enforcement experience. Rob, however, was far more interested in regenerating the market and appeasing traders than getting his pocketbook out and prosecuting them. This did not always go down well with the manager, who, having checked the market one afternoon when Rob was on duty, came back to the office disgruntled and dismayed by the disorder he'd found and quipped that 'Rob must walk down that market with blinkers on'. Rob's nickname, Blinkers, was then born. Nevertheless, he remained popular within the team and was particularly well liked among the traders.

Although Rob's attitude could have been considered to have been too laid back at times, it was and is an indication of the transition that street markets were starting to make. While markets had previously been able to operate largely unchallenged by any competition, change was imminent. The impact of shopping centres, parking controls and changing consumer expectations were to have a dramatic effect on them, and those inspectors who cared about the markets' future were well aware that the job had now to be a lot more than mere licensing and control. The role of the inspector had to be more creative, business-minded and supportive of the markets' and traders' needs. Enforcement does remain a constant and necessary arm of the borough's powers, however, and a fine balance between the two aspects of the job is always sought.

After some internal turmoil within the Tower Hamlets markets team in 2005 David Saunders took over as new head of department. His remit was to take a business approach to the markets and to resolve staffing issues. David had a military background and the air and appearance of an officer: tall, greying and with an old-style military moustache. It did not take long for the team to affectionately nickname him the Colonel, partly because of his military image and partly as a reference to the KFC fast-food chain's Colonel Sanders. The Colonel was the first manager for a considerable time who succeeded in gaining the respect not only of the team but also, perhaps more importantly, of the market traders, thus allowing new ideas in and development to take place.

David was popular with the traders, who appreciated his thoughtfulness and tolerance, but, the market being the market, he was not always beyond some friendly jousting with the occasional trader. During one visit to Whitechapel market – a large street market with a majority of Asian traders – a well-known and mischievous Turkish trader saw David approaching and stopped him to talk, commenting, 'You look like the plantation owner down here.' I don't think David was overly amused by this, but he took it in his stride, acknowledging that the marketplace was and is always a colourful experience.

During the Colonel's time in the markets team a new tranche of inspectors was employed, adding to an improving and professional team. A number of the new officers were recruited from the local community, which developed the markets' ethnic diversity in a positive manner. Numbers were increased to improve control and to adequately manage and enforce market regulations where the balance had slipped into disorder. One of the new recruits, reflecting a more diverse workforce, was market officer Abdul Goni, a young man of Bangladeshi origin. Abdul came to Britain when he was 6 years old following his father, who had migrated to Britain a year earlier in the search of a better life. Abdul, recollecting his childhood, was keen to tell me that his family struggled with poverty and racism in the East End. After sharing cramped conditions with his uncle's family, they were encouraged to squat, quite possibly with the encouragement of Terry Fitzpatrick, the 'champion of the Bengali community'. They found a suitable flat in Shadwell Gardens near Watney market.

Like many immigrants before him Abdul's father was a tailor, and both parents eked out a meagre living machining. But poverty wasn't the only issue. Racism shaped Abdul's life: in fact, 'it's changed my life, my feelings towards other human beings'. I asked Abdul what experiences he had growing up and was shocked at his answer:

> Although I remember many incidents one moment sticks out. When I was ten me and my two brothers were walking in Stepney Park when we encountered two white men. We were just walking in the park when these men went berserk and just attacked us, they could have killed us, so regardless of how things are now, better or not, I know these things still go on.

I asked Abdul how he came to be a Toby and what the role means to him:

> I struggled at school largely because I wasn't confident in English until I was twenty-five … only seven years ago. I failed all my exams but I went back to college and redid exams so eventually I got to university and passed at degree level in Business Information Systems. However, it was difficult to get work and after a few admin jobs I managed to find work with Tower Hamlets Council, which led to the inspector job. The job has been important to me as I realise that I'm one of the first Asian inspectors. I relate to the Bengali traders and understand their culture, race and poverty background.

I wanted to know if Abdul enjoys the job and if he still encounters problems with racism. He replied:

> I do really enjoy the job, there's a sense of freedom, talking and meeting people from so many different backgrounds, but I think the role is really important in the community, it gives a sense of security and identity and being an Asian inspector is particularly important as it represents the authority's side in the community. There is a great sense of respect for my role but this is mutual as I will always retain a deep sense of respect for hard-working people such as the market traders.
>
> There has [sic] been moments when I have encountered racism in the job but it's pleasing that there is now better diversity among the officers, reflecting the community.

Abdul eloquently sums up the role of the Toby: 'After all, we are here because of the traders; that's our purpose. I enjoy working in Tower Hamlets. I have been here all my life, I like playing a part in the community and working with people who are not so privileged.'

After David Saunders left his post in 2011 he was kind enough to discuss with me his thoughts on his tenure as markets head and offer thoughtful comments on markets and the role of the Toby. David had previously been assistant director at Greenwich Council and had managed front-line public services, including street markets.

David was well aware of historical issues to do with corruption and street markets, and of the negative reputation that both the markets and indeed the markets team had within the council. However, his brief within Tower Hamlets was to 'work with the traders and reverse a downward trend in their numbers and prosperity'. He realised that the strand of corruption that had run through markets was not uncommon but was a complex and difficult problem to resolve; although there had been clear cases of corruption, market officials were also open to unfair accusations: 'When a market officer is too diligent and steadfast for their taste, traders sometimes make unfounded allegations against him.

It follows, therefore, [that] traders alleging misconduct or corruption by a market officer [are] particularly mischievous and this had happened in Tower Hamlets.' David's task must have appeared quite daunting. One parking manager had commented to David that 'working in the markets was like being in war-torn Beirut'. David's reply was that he 'had served in Beirut with the British Army and the markets were actually not quite as bad, but bad enough'.

David set about the problems by improving market inspector numbers and regaining control of the markets – 'if, in fact, we had actually lost it'. He questioned the persistent 'cry' that markets were out of control (a theme I shall return to). The markets are to a degree chaotic and it is this that can make them a success, but lawlessness is another issue entirely. However, perceptions of these respective states are subjective, and misconceptions can lead to decisions taken in error.

Market officer hours were changed to cover all the opening hours of the market and to increase revenue collection. This was done by encouraging market traders to pay rent for the correct pitch space that they used. Other negotiations were made to renegotiate waste contracts and pay minimal rent for accommodation. David succeeded in turning a £400,000 deficit into a surplus after seven years in his role as head of the markets team. The other aspect of David's brief, to improve the council's relationship with market traders, was quite an undertaking, as David tended to agree with the view of the trader that the council would have been happy for the markets to close. The improved relationship with traders that David succeeded in nurturing was quite noticeable, however, to the point that one council officer remarked to David that he had 'gone native'. Admirably, David's answer to that was 'that as the traders stood in the p***ing rain to earn the money to pay my salary, I was responsible to them and only answerable to the council'. 'On my watch,' he commented, 'we never lost a market, and some, such as Brick Lane, revived.' Towards the end of David's tenure a number of councillors took a more positive view towards markets.

David regarded his role as being not only to develop the markets but also to protect them. He felt that he had successfully created an environment in his department that was geared towards 'what is in the best interest of the market' and that included the traders within it. My own belief is that he was highly successful in this: as already mentioned, he had a productive relationship with traders and the majority of his staff, being a manager who was willing to listen to suggestions and allow staff to explore those ideas, which often resulted in improvements in market and, of course, personal development. His legacy of working towards the best interests of the market by giving traders respect for and understanding of the issues that they faced in turn created a better relationship between authority and trader, thus allowing issues to be ironed out quickly and more democratically; this was surely more important for the markets than a poorly thought through physical legacy or, indeed, an ethos that failed to support the markets in a truly meaningful way.

David was wary of the council's view on the 'improvement' of markets and its continuing perception of them as a menace rather than something to take pride in. There had been historical examples where changes that had been made to markets had led only to 'blight' – in particular, at Chrisp Street and Watney markets. He said:

> For those who wanted to 'improve' the markets I had always planned to make a PowerPoint slide with a picture of crowded and successful Whitechapel market on one side and on the other a picture of a space which was clean, clear of litter, set out in orderly fashion, crime free and unpopulated by living people; and then ask the viewer which was the better street market: Whitechapel or the cemetery!

This, of course, raises the question of what 'improvement' means, and for whom. In David's view 'improvement' as commonly expressed has meant sanitisation, rather than an improved market. I will explore these themes a little later on, but at the time of writing Whitechapel market is undergoing 'improvement' works and it remains to be seen if this will lead to a successful outcome for the market. There is undoubtedly a gap between what authority sees as improvement for markets – 'gaining control' – and the controlled chaos of a hustling and bustling market. David commented that 'Brick Lane, for a short period of my time, did fulfil its ancient function as a market and permit those in great need for cash to sell whatever they could find to sell.'

Summing up his thoughts at the end of our discussion, David returned to the theme of the Toby. His experience of running the markets had taught him that the traders 'were a rich slice of humanity' and could be a 'handful for anyone', in particular the 'old white East Enders'. 'We should therefore not be too quick to question the performance of the market Toby in the past.' Having said this, there were many traders who retained his respect as 'thoroughly good men and women, frank and honest'.

David concluded by commenting on his markets team:

> … the markets team was like any other front-line team that recruits and tries to retain self-sufficient assured men and women who want to deliver public service. It certainly makes management of them interesting! Market officers work the same beat – and traders – virtually every day. Each one sets up a dynamic of their own with the traders, some maybe even going 'native'! I never doubted the Market Officers saw where their duty lay. To foster the welfare of markets and traders I have witnessed many examples of personal integrity and courage from the market officers. For their action at one really nasty incident, four team members received a commendation for bravery from the London Commissioner of Police. A police sergeant working in a market to stop illegal trading had been attacked and knocked to the ground by a gang of youths. The market officers who unhesitatingly stepped forward to protect him acted well beyond the Council's terms of employment but not, I think, their own.

As a testament to David's work in the team the market department was rewarded for its success, winning best team in Tower Hamlets in 2008, which was a source of pride for officers and market traders alike.

The end of the Toby

By 2012 it was clear that the economic recession was going to have an enormous impact on various departments within the council as it sought to save money while still seeking to improve and get best value out of the services it provides. The market team was no exception and underwent a restructure. The priorities were to have a more 'visible' service to tackle crime and anti-social behaviour, and it was decided that generic enforcement officers would represent a better use of resource to tackle a multitude of issues.

The market officer's job thus changed, morphing into a generic role that saw the end of the market officer title. The team amalgamated with the Tower Hamlets Enforcement Officers (THEOs) and became 'THEO markets and enforcement'. In what might be seen as a return to a previous age, the officers would be in a high-profile uniform and the emphasis would be on greater 'control' and enforcement in the markets – paradoxically, perhaps, mirroring the Tobys of older generations.

It remains to be seen what the impact of this new look and direction will be for the team and the markets. Although the majority of our job is still managing and controlling the markets, it is clear that for the present it is the end of the Toby, but not of enforcement and control within the borough's street markets. The fluid balance of power between authority and trader seems set to continue and issues around market development and 'improvement' remain contentious and debatable. Posterity will no doubt tell us how it views the 'success' of street markets in the twenty-first century.

Above and below: Wentworth Street, 1938: early photographs of one of the first Tobys. (Courtesy of Tower Hamlets Local History Library & Archives)

Trader revolt

Petticoat Lane increased in size and popularity with its new found legitimacy after 1894, but this only intensified the demand for the best pitches. With no governing regulations in place to sufficiently control the market fighting among traders became commonplace, creating an untenable situation. Peter Rexter, in a newspaper article dated 1894 describing the history of the 'Lane' at the time, writes: 'The lane was becoming a beehive for street traders: so many in fact that men fought each other for pitches or nearly broke their necks in a mad scramble to secure positions.' In *The People of the Abyss*, Jack London describes the hardships he witnessed: 'For here, in the East End, the obscenities and brute vulgarities of life are rampant. There is no privacy. The bad corrupts the good, and all fester together.' There is no doubt that Petticoat Lane and its surrounding area was a breeding ground for criminal activity, with gangs of thieves, child labour, prostitution and exploitation.

This period of unrest can also be seen in the context of the general poverty in the East End and, in particular, the Jewish struggle towards political recognition and the vote and improvement in living conditions for Jew and gentile alike. In the 1920s most Jewish people in the East End were classed as aliens and, as a result, were excluded from the electoral register. A common unity was arrived at between Jews and non-Jews to form unions in what became an increasing radicalisation of the East End. Affiliations were particularly strong with the Labour Party and the Communists. Although the market traders of Petticoat Lane did not form a strong union, as some workforces did, they did unite under the leadership of Abraham Valentine, a street traders' leader, forming a street traders' association. Having been a liberal councillor, Valentine switched his alliance to the Labour Party in 1919; later, he became president of the Whitechapel and Spitalfields Costermongers Union in 1927 and helped secure stability for the traders when, under the General Powers Act, Stepney Borough Council began to regulate the market and license the traders.

Trading restrictions were another major area of Christian concern. Yet, much as one person wanted to buy and another wanted to sell, Christians felt obliged to stop them from doing so on a Sunday. In England the Church supported the Sunday Trading Restriction Bill in 1928, as they had supported every attempt to retain Sunday trading restrictions since the Sunday

Fairs Act of 1448. But the public mood had now changed and, as the markets were largely populated by Jews, it was essential that trade could take place on a Sunday, to avoid the Jewish Sabbath (Saturday): the strict observance of rites meant that Jews could do no work on that day. Sunday trading was finally accepted after years of struggle on the part of market traders and others which resulted in the Shops (Sunday Trading Restriction) Act of 1936. This legislation attempted compromise, but, according to one commentator, 'succeeded in making the law a laughing stock for decades. It became legal to sell tins of clotted cream on a Sunday, but not evaporated milk. It was legal to sell fuel for cars, but not for cigarette lighters. It was legal to sell razors to cut corns with, but not to shave with (www.badnewsaboutchristianity.com). Despite these peculiarities and contradictions, however, it was still a major breakthrough for the market traders of Petticoat Lane.

The efforts towards the Act on the part of the market traders was led largely by trader Mike Stern. Aside from his achievements as a market trader representative, Stern was a remarkable market character and in the days when it was fashionable for traders to

Petticoat Lane on Sunday morning, c.1910.
(Courtesy of Tower Hamlets Local History Library & Archives)

The greatest Sunday market in the world: Petticoat Lane, c.1920.
(Courtesy of Bishopsgate Institute)

dress up to attract customers he donned warlike Native American
feathered headgear. Famous for his market patter and knowledge
of Shakespeare, when selling his wares he could be heard to
say, for example: 'Oh when I am dead and forgotten, as I shall
be, and sleep in dull cold marble with these lovely Utility towels,
ten bob a pair.' Aside from the battle fought for Sunday trading,
Stern also campaigned successfully against the Food Hygiene
Markets Act 1966, which sought to insist that all food stalls should
have sinks for washing and proposed heavy fines. Stern was by all
accounts regarded as a father figure within the market and spent
fifty years as the president of the Federation of Street Traders
Union (later the Street Traders Association) before retiring in
1972. Other battles hard won by the Street Traders Association,
which had become a formidable interest group, included that
against proposals for a 300-shop arcade in Middlesex Street.
The *East London Advertiser* reported in 1959 the traders' sentiments on this matter: 'Leave the Lane alone … Why spoil it
with shops … the colourful street market will die if plans go ahead
for a 300 shop arcade … putting the mockers on the market is the

city and county properties, they want to spend £200,000 towards the Lanes' funeral.'

Market traders had thus not only won the battle with the authorities over their concern with the Lane's reputation for crime and mayhem but had also fought the Christian ethics of the time. Both represented major steps forward for the market and for its legal status, helping to enshrine its place in the East End. The market, now famed and, moreover, protected, would develop into London's – and perhaps the world's – most successful street market. Its success would have an enormous impact on the local community as it became a popular tourist attraction, creating an economic boom in the area.

Mock auctions

A confidence trick and menace that proliferated in the markets of Petticoat Lane and Brick Lane was the mock auction. Such 'auctioneers' would set themselves up on the peripheries of the market on private land or in vacant shops and would very often capture the attention of the public. Not all 'auctions' were cons, and many traders and members of the public claimed that a great many auctioneers were law-abiding: they enjoyed the sense of drama and fun they brought to the markets. However, the over-riding historical evidence is that most were 'mock auctioneers'.

The silver-tongued 'auctioneers' were experts in their craft and always used the same techniques to relieve punters of their money. The basic operation includes five simple stages. First, the auctioneer captures the attention of his audience, usually through the use of a loudhailer, and presents high-value goods which, he says, will be sold for rock-bottom prices. Then, to soften up the audience, he gives away worthless articles and presents a mystery package which is sold very cheaply. The crucial part of the con begins when the 'auctioneer' sells genuine articles to members of his gang, who are planted within the crowd.

The crowd is then hooked and frantic bidding starts to secure the bargains. Finally, the main swindle is executed, in which worthless goods are disguised as the genuine article and sold for a considerable sum of money. The auctioneer usually wraps up the sale by adding a sweetener freebie gift to the bag of worthless goods that the punter has, unwittingly, purchased.

I witnessed such auctions regularly in Petticoat Lane and Brick Lane shortly after becoming a market inspector in the mid-1990s. The experience left me quite unnerved, but I was also mesmerised by the skill of the auctioneers. During one such auction in Brick Lane about ten years ago an auctioneer was 'selling' laptops and televisions. When sold to the public they looked like the genuine article, sealed inside the appropriate manufacturers' boxes. One unfortunate customer told me that, having thought he'd got the bargain of a lifetime, he went home, opened his box and made the unpleasant discovery of bricks inside instead of a TV.

The gangs were, of course, aware of the presence of the market inspectors but were by and large not concerned; as they were on private ground they were out of our jurisdiction and could be tackled only by the police or trading standards officers. Members of the public were often too frightened to come forward and complain as the gangs threatened violence towards anyone who interfered with their activities. The *East London Advertiser* of February 1961 reported the crusade of a tailor from Petticoat Lane called Harry Davis against mock auction cons in Petticoat Lane. Evidently Harry would hand out letters to the public warning them of the con, in return receiving threats from the auctioneers that he would be not only beaten up but also 'slashed'. At one point he received a letter saying 'stop interfering or we'll get a stooge to say you have been assaulting women in the crowd'. Harry's crusade was thankfully taken up by Parliament and the introduction of a bill to get rid of mock auctions was followed up by the Mock Auctions Act of 1961. This was only partially successful in its aims but was followed by two or three other consumer protection acts and finally consolidated in the statutory instrument Consumer Protection from Unfair Trading Regulations 2008. Mock auctions have now finally cleared from the markets but are occasionally still to be seen in shop outlets in Oxford Street or Tottenham Court Road.

War years

Petticoat Lane and Brick Lane continued to flourish during the Second World War despite the very difficult circumstances of people who lived in the East End of London. Ironically, however, this period opened up opportunities for many people to become market traders, as many were unable to enlist owing to poor health or age restrictions. Market trading became the perfect job for many people.

Doctor, from *Sphere* magazine, 1945. (Courtesy of Mary Evans Picture Library)

Escapologist, from *Sphere* magazine, 1945. (Courtesy of Mary Evans Picture Library)

Those who could not fight worked long days and also undertook civilian duties such as 'fire watching' in an effort to 'do their bit' for the war effort. Day-to-day lives were hard and monotonous, from which the Sunday markets provided a welcome respite; in fact, for the people of the East End there was little else to do but visit the market. The war restricted travel and many people were even scared to visit the cinema for fear of being bombed. Many welcomed the reprieve of a day out at the market and an opportunity to spend their money, as it afforded one of the few opportunities to do so, there being no restaurants or holidays in which people could indulge.

Enormous commodity restrictions were put in place during and after the war years. In particular, food was rationed and coupons were used in exchange for goods. The main trade in the market was, of course, in food items and second-hand clothing. Traders would source the latter from pawnbrokers and jumble sales and found very inventive ways in which to source food: for example, a market trader recollecting the war years (recorded for sound archives for the Imperial War Museum) remembers a trader in Petticoat Lane 'pulling a stroke' in selling simulated honeycomb on his stall. This 'honeycomb' was made by pouring golden syrup into his bath and mixing it with bicarbonate of soda. Other items which were in short supply, such as stockings, might also be obtained through the market.

Examples of foodstuffs directly restricted because of the war were fruit – only home-grown produce could be bought – and fish, restricted because wet fish was deep-sea caught. Additionally, some seafood was also restricted, particularly prawns, which were caught off the Norwegian coast. This meant that cockles, winkles and shrimp caught in estuaries were widely sold on 'seafood' stalls within the markets. However, the black market in commodities made up shortfalls in the goods that people required. The importance of coupons in obtaining goods and a great demand for the most sought-after commodities (butter, meat and the market's speciality of second-hand clothing) inevitably led to

a black market in coupons, but unless they were stolen from local
authorities traders frowned upon illicit ration books, knowing
the hardship that their theft would have caused. Traders made a
very good living during the war and, by and large, worked closely
with each other, but there is evidence of rivalry, as revealed in

Spellbound young fan, from *Sphere* magazine, 1945.
(Courtesy of Mary Evans Picture Library)

Haberdasher, from *Sphere* magazine, 1945. (Courtesy of Mary Evans Picture Library)

a Stepney committee report from 1943: 'Owing to war circumstances and the restriction of supplies of food, hardship is being caused to street traders licensed for vegetables only in competing with persons who are licensed to sell both fruit and vegetables.' This comment illustrates not only the food shortages caused by the war but, as explored previously, difficulties with contentious rules relating to street trading licences.

Committee reports show that while the market was regulated and traders were warned and prosecuted for breaches of licence conditions, the market continued to function even under war rationing and food shortages. Indeed, it thrived, serving as it did as a necessity for local residents eager for goods in short supply; it was very much at the heart of the East End community's survival during the war.

Planning and development

In the Victorian period a great number of London's street markets came under threat of closure. Those at Tottenham Court Road, Aldgate and Caledonian Road and markets within Camden were removed to build tramlines or because of road traffic obstruction. These markets simply disappeared or moved to quieter side streets. Shopping habits also began to change: West End department stores began to flourish, as did chains of grocery shops.

The costermonger survived, however, owing to an increased population of Jewish and Irish people who had started new lives in the East End of London. Jewish populations fleeing the pogroms and the Irish the potato famine made their way to New York and London. Their contributions to the market saw it strengthen its position in the East End of London; indeed, visitors began to come from far and wide to experience shopping in the renowned 'Lane'.

The market, as noted, was still a major concern for the authorities and as early as 1926 plans were made to remodel the 'quaint' Petticoat Lane. Tenement buildings were to be demolished in Middlesex Street and to be replaced with upmarket shops. The idea was to transform the 'cheap'-looking Petticoat Lane into the Regent Street of the East End. Areas were cleared, but this aim remained fanciful. In 1943 the County of London Plan shows that street markets such as Petticoat Lane were thought of as impractical; at this time the intention was to move them into small squares adjacent to the streets in which they had formerly been held. Some markets, such as Covent Garden, were moved at this time, but the Petticoat Lane market, as ever, was impervious to change and continued to occupy the same large sprawl of streets that it always had.

The Blitz of the Second World War devastated large areas of the East End of London: many homes and other buildings were destroyed. The markets and areas surrounding Petticoat Lane were no exception and, indeed, photographs of the time show large-scale destruction, particularly in Middlesex Street, leaving large areas of derelict and damaged land. Post-war planning and rebuilding projects were essential for the redevelopment of blitzed areas.

Market traders faced a further threat in 1959 in the form of a plan for a new covered shopping arcade in Middlesex Street. The proposal was sold as a replacement for the quiet market winter trading that would provide a fresh attraction and redevelop areas still bomb-damaged. Unsurprisingly, however, the plan did not find favour with the market traders; in particular, temporary traders knew that their livelihood could be in jeopardy as their street trading licences could be withdrawn at any time. Fortunately the plan did not come to fruition and trade continued in earnest. Further development of the area was less controversial; new offices and shops were erected but the market was left to trade uncontested.

Petticoat Lane has remained in a period of flux ever since. The market, having been 'saved' from development, is now perhaps at the mercy of future modification. As less importance is placed upon the street market and with traders exercising less power, future developers may be successful in redeveloping in a manner deleterious to the market but, equally, without development Petticoat Lane could be lost forever. It remains to be seen what planning and development will mean for the Lane in the early years of the new millennium.

A lane of nations

They came to here from everywhere
'Tis they that made dis city strong.
A world of food displayed on streets
Where all the world can come and dine
On meals that end with bitter sweets
And cultures melt and intertwine,
Two hundred languages give voice

To fifteen thousand changing years
And all religions can rejoice
With exiled souls and pioneers.
I love dis overcrowded place.

Extract from 'The London Breed', by Benjamin Zephaniah

Immigration in the East End has a long and fascinating history, particularly in terms of its influence on London's development as one of the most significant cities in the world. Such influence began on the streets and pavements of London's markets, the most important of which was Petticoat Lane. Immigrants' motives for coming to London were generally similar: to flee persecution and poverty and to achieve self-advancement and perhaps wealth; and, as with many immigration histories, settlement in the East End of London was not an easy passage.

Both Petticoat Lane and Brick Lane owe their existence and development to the two foremost migrations of the seventeenth century, those of the French Huguenots, and the nineteenth-century influxes of Russian and European Jews fleeing the Russian pogroms and other discrimination. Among the Jews fleeing tyranny were Russian and German radicals who did much to instigate radical politics within the East End. Future Communist leaders Leon Trotsky and Vladimir Lenin were among those who made close connections with the local Labour Party in the East End. Another radical was Peter Kropotkin, who helped form the anarchist Freedom Press in Whitechapel. This still exists to this day, operating from a small premises in Angel Alley, and its activists still regularly attend Brick Lane market, where they distribute a radical newspaper and glower at the authority of market inspectors. One edition of this newspaper, disconcertedly, featured anti-market inspector sentiments.

The third major influx of new people was from Ireland, in the wake of the potato famine, as noted above. In the late 1800s the immigrant population was particularly high. William J. Fishman, in his book *East End 1888*, comments on how the different ethnic groups co-existed: the older Dutch Jews were indistinguishable from the cockneys; Russian Jews formed their own separate community and followed their own trades; Germans settlers, who were held in high esteem, also specialised in particular trades but worked alongside other East Europeans and Irish settlers in something approaching the classic 'melting pot'. Fishman also points out, however, the high levels of endemic poverty and the difficulties the immigrants faced, with open hostility from 'native' Englishmen who considered that the Jews were 'driving out the English from Wentworth Street to Mile End'. Charles Booth also reported that newcomers had gradually replaced the English population in whole districts that were formerly outside the Jewish quarter. Formerly in Whitechapel, Commercial Street roughly divided the Jewish areas of Petticoat Lane and Goulston Street.

Anti-Jewish sentiment was a common response to the influxes of new people, the 'alien invasion' of London being blamed for many of the city's ills. In particular, the Ripper killings in 1888 whipped up a frenzy of discrimination in which many blamed a 'Jew' for the atrocities and for other problems associated with the East End. Even existing Jewish communities were hostile to new Jewish immigrants, with the Jewish Board of Guardians organising the repatriation of thousands of Jewish immigrants from 1881 to 1906. It is ironic and shameful that many who fled persecution, famine and disease had to endure further extreme hardships in their country of refuge. It is to those newcomers' great credit that they would not only help to change the face of the East End of London but would, in some cases, come to shape the nation in fields such as politics, entertainment, science and the arts.

The poverty and poor living conditions at this time in the East End are well documented. Dorset Street, a street away from Petticoat Lane, was hailed at one time as the worst street in London. Fiona Rule's book *The Worst Street in London* aptly describes the slum conditions endured by the families who dwelt in the homes there, with as many as six or seven adults and children crowding one room at No. 25 Dorset Street. These conditions, made worse by unscrupulous landlords, drove the population to desperate means of survival. Prostitution was rife, as Fiona Rule notes: 'Many of the local prostitutes were rather pathetic, gin-soaked women whose alcoholism had caused their families to abandon them many years earlier. Most were in their forties and possessed rapidly fading looks.' This rather sad description is all the more telling and disturbing when the conditions of poverty and prostitution that are still very much present in today's East End streets are considered: descriptions of prostitutes from the late 1800s could easily apply to those of the present day. In those same streets can still be seen women plying their trade before returning to their squats to sleep away the day, their tired, haggard appearance and bloodshot eyes betraying the destructiveness of alcohol and drugs. Battered and lonely, these women are as desperate in the twenty-first century as they were in the nineteenth.

The area around Petticoat Lane, in particular, plays an integral role in the story; it is probable that those prostitutes murdered during this period relied upon the markets as a source of income, and it was a costermonger, Louis Diemshutz, who discovered the body of Elizabeth Stride, the Ripper's fifth victim, in Berner Street, close to Commercial Street and the market. As mentioned above, Goulston Street, part of the main 'drag' of Petticoat Lane, is the site of the notorious graffiti written on a wall above part of Catherine Eddowes' garments (the location is now a fish and chip shop). The police destroyed this evidence, presumably because of fears that it would incite anti-Semitic unrest. The murders not only caused alarm in society at large but did nothing to help the burgeoning communities within the East End, with Huguenots, Jews and Irish blaming each other for their various misfortunes.

The legacy of these murders lingers in the form of 'Jack the Ripper tourism', which has been cashed in on locally in a variety of ways. The Ripper memorabilia of The Ten Bells has already been described, and The Bell, on the corner of New Goulston Street

and Middlesex Street, in which the last Whitechapel victim,
Frances Coles, was seen drinking on 12 February 1891 with James
Sadler shortly before she was murdered, is decorated in a dark,
gothic fashion, playing on this aspect of its history; it even goes so
far as to display advertisements such as 'Try the Ripper's favourite
tipple – a "Slippery Nipple"'. Several pubs with connections to the
murder victims have returned to their original names after periods
under other appellations; thus The Bell was The Market Trader
from 1997 to 2009, while The Princess Alice, on the junction of
Wentworth Street and Commercial Street, in which the same
Frances Coles was also seen drinking, was for a time known as
The City Darts, but was changed back to its earlier name after a
makeover in 2005.

What is certain is that the East End has had to overcome the
huge challenges of poverty, crime, disease and discrimination it
faced in order to survive. The market provided needed commerce,
community and spirit to assist the needs of the poor.

However, the 1901 census reveals that the typical picture
was of hard-working immigrant families living and working on
Petticoat Lane in honest professions. Levy Barnett and his wife
Rachel were both born in Germany and at the time of the census
were both in their fifties. Levy's occupation was listed as tailor
and his wife's as costermonger. They had three sons: Abraham,
aged 22, Philip, aged 30, and Jack, aged 32. All were costermongers. They also had five daughters between the ages of 14 and 24:
three were cigarette makers, one was a housemaid and the other
was still at school – showing that at least a modicum of education
was available to families of this social status. All the children were
born in Aldgate, so the parents must have come to these shores
in their early twenties, probably fleeing oppression. They lived at
No. 7 Artillery Passage, very close to Petticoat Lane, and, judging
by the head of the household's profession, they perhaps had a
head start in their new life, with the ability to offer a service and
sell their own wares within the market. We do not know what all
of the family members sold but the number involved within the

market as costermongers shows how reliant immigrants could be
on the market – but also that they must have been moderately
economically successful, as they were able to send their youngest
daughter to school.

Negative representations of the Jewish community were
common throughout the period, one of which, in particular,
has close associations with Petticoat Lane market. The character Fagan, in Charles Dickens' *Oliver Twist*, is immortalised
as a stereotypical Jew, sending the young onto the streets to
pickpocket for him. Dickens based Fagan on a real criminal
character, Isaac 'Ikey' Solomon, who lived in Bell Lane,
a market street within Petticoat Lane. (Hardly coincidently,
pickpocketing and theft still remain a problem in the markets to
this day.) Dickens' defence of the portrayal centred around the
argument that the character was a true reflection of the criminal
underbelly: the author himself had nothing against the Jewish
faith. This may have been true, but it is perhaps an unfortunate
by-product of his talents as a writer that the Fagan character is
so memorable and persuasive as the archetype criminal Jew.
There were, of course, significant negative portrayals of Jews
previously in literature – such was embedded in English and
literary consciousness – the most famous of which, perhaps,
is Shakespeare's Shylock in *The Merchant of Venice*. Shakespeare,
at least, is unlikely to have been familiar with Jews, and was
simply repeating the widely believed stereotype: but the same
cannot be said for Dickens.

Of course, the Jewish community would not be the only
immigrants to suffer from the xenophobic attitudes of England's
indigenous – or more long-standing – inhabitants. Future immigrant communities for generations would be subject to similar
racism, notably directed towards the Irish, black and Caribbean
communities and, more recently, towards Eastern Europeans and
the Muslim community. Many of these communities settling in
the East End are continuing a long tradition of survival in and
around the marketplaces of Petticoat Lane and Brick Lane.

The Aliens Act of 1905 institutionalised the idea that immigrants were to blame for deteriorating living and working conditions and sought to end further immigration – particularly Jewish – rather than tackling the obvious social problems, at the root of which were often the exploitations of the ruling classes. But the sheer capacity for survival and the continuing poverty in the East End ensured that the market would stay firmly affixed as an anchor for the communities of the East End, both at the time and later, when new waves of immigration followed. Many Pakistanis, Indians and Bangladeshis made this area their home and, later, after the Second World War, people from the Caribbean arrived on the *Empire Windrush* to help rebuild Britain. Turkish and Afghan people have also settled and, more recently, Somalians and economic migrants from Eastern Europe have found their way to the street markets of Petticoat Lane, Brick Lane and Whitechapel.

By the end of the nineteenth century and the beginning of the twentieth the market positively reflected its community through the various foods sold within the market. An article in *The Illustrated News* of 1893 describes Passover Eve in Petticoat Lane:

> Stout young Jewesses in seal skin jackets and diamonds look with watering mouths at the fat green Spanish olives and the rich Dutch pickled cucumbers in Assenheim's window; shrivelled old Jewesses in poor shawls and hideous plastered wigs gather round the stalls with the special crockery ware and the bitter herbs and the balls of chopped almonds.

Jewish delis and restaurants became renowned within the area, notably Mark's Deli and, particularly, Bloom's Restaurant, famous for its smoked salmon. Bloom's was founded by Morris Bloom. Originally located in Brick Lane, it moved first to Montague Street and then to Whitechapel. Changing demographics led to its closure in 1996 and, sadly, it was replaced by a Burger King fast-food restaurant.

In an article from *Picture Postcard Monthly* in 1994, in which a local man called Ikey Jacobs fondly remembers his boyhood spent in 1920s Petticoat Lane, he focuses in particular upon the varied food stall experiences, including 'Polly Nathan's "far famed" fish shop'. 'Fanny Marks gutted, skinned and sliced up Dutch herrings … hot salt beef sandwiches, stale bread sold to the poor, hot roasted monkey nuts, cold wet fish' – sold by Ikey Bogard (a character I will explore shortly) – and 'The original Joe Assenheim's of 56 Storey Lane, still dispensed ice cream out of the freezer on his barrow to the cry of "penny half, tuppence whole one".' The article also mentions Tubby Isaacs, on the corner of Goulston Street, who sold jellied eels. The Tubby Isaacs stall started trading in 1919 and, now in its fourth generation as a family run business, remains at the same site to this day. Ikey Jacobs sums up his thoughts about the market:

> The lane; then with its many shops, stalls and itinerants was indeed a melting pot of chanting and bantering characters using Yiddish, Russian and Polish, not to mention back slang to extol the virtues of the goods on offer – I'm pretty sure of one thing – I'll never see its like again.

Food is now once again a major feature of Petticoat Lane market, in particular on weekdays in Goulston Street, where food has played a part in the street's revival. Modern food stalls sell food from all nations: here you can buy Chinese dim sum, Mediterranean falafel wraps, vegan Caribbean-inspired stews and curries, Caribbean jerk chicken, Thai curries and American-style sticky ribs. The food reflects not only the nationalities of the people selling it but the country's growing appetite for world food; here it sells mostly to local upwardly mobile office workers.

Away from food, other items also reflected the various communities. A famous brand, Lee Cooper jeans, was started in a rundown factory in Middlesex Street in 1908 by Morris Cooper

Tourist postcard showing Bloom's Restaurant. (Courtesy of the Jewish Museum)

and Louis Maister. By all accounts, Petticoat Lane offered very good-quality goods with a wide range of choices. Especially popular were men's suits, which could be purchased at far cheaper prices than in the shops. Often stallholders had tailoring shops behind or close to their stalls, into which customers would be shown to be measured up; the following Sunday they could pick up a bespoke tailored suit. Unfortunately most of the tailoring shops have now gone and the high-quality merchandise previously evident on many stalls has generally been replaced by cheaper items imported from China. There are also, of course, more stalls that reflect the large Asian community now present, with saris and other Asian garments a common sight. Nonetheless, the market still has a wide variety of additional goods for sale, which now include mobile phone accessories, watches, jewellery, shoes, luggage and household accessories.

Man with a big chest, Petticoat Lane.
(Courtesy of Tower Hamlets Local History Library & Archives)

The world-famous Petticoat Lane

Petticoat Lane is a cause for celebration and should be lauded as a cultural and historical site as important as St Paul's Cathedral, the Tower of London or the British Museum. Its significance cannot be overstated: its legacy is London's inheritance, its bitter struggle and hardships are London and its people. The market, although continuing to struggle with various issues, was to have a golden age that no other market or shopping experience probably anywhere in the world could come close to matching.

The market's heyday stretched from the post-war years up to the late 1980s, when it expanded beyond Middlesex Street and Wentworth Street into New Goulston Street, Goulston Street, Bell Lane, Strype Street, Leyden Street, Old Castle Street and Toynbee Street, with approximately 1,400 stalls every Sunday. Although it was not on the same scale during the weekdays, the market was still very busy within Wentworth, Goulston and Toynbee Streets. On Sundays the market drew vast crowds: it was a must-see attraction for tourists and general public alike, who were drawn in by the mystic and legend of the Lane. The streets were filled with a huge assortment of stalls, each pathway and turning leading to yet more, crammed like sardines. The crowds would move at a snail's pace, their eyes being drawn to one temptation or another. The appeal for the market trader was that they did not have to wait for potential customers, as a shop's owner would; the world would pass by their stall as they waited, and they could attract their customers with clever patter and magnetic personalities. Awaiting the public would be an array of men's and women's clothing, shoes and bed linen, tourist artefacts, jewellery, kitchen utensils, crockery, records, toys, luggage and many different foods, the scents from which tantalised the senses.

Personalities
The market is really about the people who inhabit it – not just the traders and customers but also the other varied and extraordinary souls who make the marketplace their home or their haunt:

the beggars, prostitutes, thieves, rig men, drug addicts, spiffs, actors, celebrities, artists and con men.

On a typical day spent on the Lane I am always perpetually absorbed by its steady stream of eccentric personalities. In the early hours are the sex workers, making their way homewards, perhaps with the final punter or their pimp. Always desperate-looking and eager for alcohol and drugs, they shatter the quiet morning air with their raucous disquiet. They are soon replaced by the early traders coming in to set up their stalls; recently that's been the Khan brothers, who sell delicious curry from their mobile stall. A likeable pair, always smiling, they never miss a cheerful morning's greeting. It is an uplifting start to the day. As the day progresses and more traders arrive, at some point I will see Mr Sharma, who shakes my hand and always says his catchphrase – indeed, it is now his nickname among the inspectors – 'cup of tea, cup of coffee'. With a polite refusal, it is onwards with business. Terry and George, two good friends on the market who are of Turkish and English descent, are purveyors of ladies' garments. I always enjoy listening to the banter between them. The theme is usually football, as one supports Manchester United and the other Liverpool. I – supporting Liverpool – am sometimes caught up in the debate and foolishly I will take a guess as to who will win the league. Unfortunately it is always Terry's prediction that is the most accurate – as Manchester United have finished ahead of Liverpool with depressing regularity for many years now. The pair contributes much between them to the atmosphere of the market.

Weaving in and out of the stalls is a proud transvestite wearing an alluring ladies' business outfit but with an appallingly ill-fitting blonde wig, stocky legs and broad hands that easily give away the secret. The traders hardly turn a hair but do occasionally shake their heads and smile at the brazen exhibitionism of it all. Following on are the London Walks groups who have come to stare at vestiges of Ripper history. I am reminded of something Tom Hunter said about East End gentrification: 'it is in danger of becoming a Jack the Ripper museum.' Office workers congregate at the food stalls at lunch time, mingling and feasting on the various foods on offer. In the afternoon Nigerian women in the most colourful garments visit the market seeking great quantities of clothes and luggage to take back 'home'. Not a day goes by without some arguing, some laughter, and a few cat-and-mouse games played with traffic wardens; all of life is enacted in the market arena.

Market trader Joe Barnett, a respected member of the market who has worked in Petticoat Lane for over fifty years, told me how he fondly remembers the golden era of Petticoat Lane:

> When I got a stall in Middlesex Street on Sunday it was like winning the pools, as I had to wait for years for a licence from the waiting list. Twenty to thirty years ago the market was packed with tourists and so busy that stalls were nearly turned over by the amount of people coming through the market. All the side streets were also packed; it was wonderful.
>
> Wages were very good in those days; you would never miss a Sunday. I remember one Sunday I was so excited to get to the market, coming out of my house I slipped down the stairs and broke my toe but I still went to the market, just bandaged up the toe. It was just too good to miss.
>
> I know things have to change but [I] don't enjoy it anymore. The Lane was well known all over the world; pearly queens would come out, Prince Monolulu would come through the market with his walking stick and fancy clothes shouting, 'Petticoat Lane, the famous Petticoat Lane, come to Petticoat Lane.' Middlesex Street at the beginning [the city end] had a monkey and organ grinder and parrots created a great atmosphere. Now parking has killed the markets off but I loved the markets in the good days, I had great times and a lot of good friends and I'm upset by what's been lost.

Ras Prince Monolulu, whom Joe mentions, was born in 1881 in London and was of West Indian descent. His real name was Peter Carl Mackay. He rose to fame when he picked the winner of the 1920 Epsom Derby at outside odds of 100–6 and won £8,000, an enormous amount of money at that time. He appeared in newsreels and at race-courses around the country, where he would sell tips, and became the most renowned black man in Britain. Widely known for his flamboyant attire, he would wear an elaborate headdress of ostrich feathers, a colourful cloak and gaiters, a colossal scarf wrapped around his waist and was always with his huge shooting stick-cum-umbrella. He appeared in many British films, including *I Gotta Horse* with Billy Fury. Prince Monolulu's other favourite pastime was to pitch up in Petticoat Lane market, and also sometimes Brick Lane market, where he would pass off racing tips in brown envelopes, shouting his catchphrase 'I gotta horse, I gotta horse!'. He died in bizarre circumstances in 1965, choking on a strawberry-filled chocolate.

Possibly the most famous sight of all in Petticoat Lane was the legendary plate thrower Gerald Strong, whose father Sidney was renowned for his auctioneering skills. Gerald, with a crowd gathering around him, would throw china tea sets balanced on top of dinner sets up into the air and skilfully catch them again. To many people I speak to regarding Petticoat Lane, Gerald is perhaps their most compelling and pleasurable memory. Gerald Strong was not the only character in the post-war period; a local resident, Laurie Allen, who lived in Goulston Street, recalls various odd personalities (Bishopsgate Voices: www.bishopsgate.org.uk): a man who would parade three monkeys on his arm and place them on top of your head or shoulder so that for a few pence you could take a picture; the famous Peanut Queen; a character named Mary Green, who was not known for her cleanliness; and a lady known as Monkey Mille who 'wasn't the greatest of lookers, but [a] wonderful person'.

Another famous – or perhaps infamous – character in Petticoat Lane was Ikey Bogard, whose nickname (from a time not enlightened by political correctness) I have elected to omit here. Ikey Jacobs, in his recollections in *Picture Postcard Monthly* from June 1984, recalls Bogard, the local gangster, who 'still sold wet fish when not engaged in nefarious exploits'. He was a dark-skinned Jewish man with black curly hair. By all accounts he was an eccentric personality who used to dress and parade around in a cowboy outfit, complete with a gun placed in his trousers. He supplemented his

market trade with a career as a pimp and 'hard man' for the gangster
Arthur Harding, a predecessor to Jack Spot and the Krays, who grew
up in the area near Bethnal Green known as the 'Old Nichol', one
of the worst Victorian slums. (The life of Arthur Harding will be
explored further on page 148/9.) Bogard's career landed him in jail
for punching a policeman, but in the First World War he won the
military medal for bravery and afterwards, in peacetime, he turned
his life away from crime and eventually even worked for the police.

A far more infamous gangster was 'Jack Spot', born Jacob
Comacho, the son of Jewish Polish immigrants, in 1912. He grew
up in the East End near Brick Lane and followed Arthur Harding
into a criminal career. Unfortunately for traders in Petticoat Lane,
after occupation at the age of 15 as a runner for a bookie he quickly
elevated his career to a role aiding a protection racket. The 1930s
were difficult times economically for traders and Jack Spot
exploited their fears of new stallholders coming in and diluting
their takings. He made sure that he was an off-putting, menacing
presence. He was also fond of card trick cons such as 'take the pick'
and, like fruit hanging from low branches, the Lane provided easy
pickings in this regard. In addition, he was also responsible for
establishing protection rackets in Brick Lane, 'protecting' shopkeepers and traders from the fascists, who had targeted Brick Lane,
like Petticoat Lane, because of its large Jewish populace.

Jack Spot was extremely effective at his brutal 'profession' and
quickly outgrew his senior partner, setting himself up as the
self-styled 'King of Aldgate'. He went some way to redeeming
himself, however, by allegedly fighting against Oswald Mosley's
fascists in the famous battle of Cable Street, where he is reputed
to have received a severe beating from a policeman. In later years
his empire declined, but he had maintained a grip over a large
part of the East End for more than thirty years.

More widely famous names that have been associated with the
Lane include Warren and David Gold, who started the boutique
'Lord John' and were at the cutting edge of fashion in swinging
sixties London. They had a number of shops that sold clothes to

the rich and the famous but their roots lay in Petticoat Lane, where they started their trade, and despite their wealth and fame they still liked to work Sunday mornings on the market. They would turn up at Petticoat Lane at 5.30 a.m. as typical enthusiastic traders, but in flamboyant style used the headlights of their Rolls-Royce to illuminate their leather coats to prospective customers. Prominent businessman and television personality Alan Sugar, too, started his career in Petticoat Lane, selling electrical goods.

One of the most renowned personalities within Petticoat Lane over the last thirty years is stall provider Mr Benny Banks. Known simply as Benny, he runs his business from a location in Leyden Street, opposite the old chicken factory, which has now been torn down to make way for modern apartments. When I first arrived on the market I was quickly introduced to Benny and his sons, who helped him operate his business. He was a lithe, tall man, perhaps not formally educated but certainly no one's dupe; generally he was calm and pleasant, but at other times, when his temper was lost, you would suddenly be face to face with a true hardened character of the East End.

Benny played a pivotal role in the running of the market, not only providing rigs to traders but placing them on the correct pitches. This was no easy feat as on a Sunday in Petticoat Lane hundreds of traders could be involved. A large part of the donkey work would be done the day before by vagabonds hired by Benny. The most taxing work, however, was completed by Benny and his sons on the Sunday morning, when casual traders would need a rig, and this task could be completed only when the inspectors had finished allocating the pitches. As I have already described, the allocation of pitches on a Sunday morning was a tense and volatile situation, which was only exacerbated by the frustration of Benny and his sons, who were desperate to get rigs placed on the market and their job completed.

Benny fought a long legal battle with Tower Hamlets Council over rig storage and the size of stalls, extending over twenty years dating back to 1980. Local residents, who were fed-up with Benny's rigs being left on the public footway, put pressure on the council for them to be moved. Benny, who only had his site in Leyden Street, was able to store only 350 stalls and was forced to leave the remaining 150 stalls on the street. Attempts were made to obtain new premises but these were refused on the grounds of noise. Benny feared that he would be issued notice on those rigs left out on the public footway, which would have a devastating impact upon his business and the market, as his rigs were 'the backbone of the 200-year-old market' (*East London Advertiser*, 11 February 1983). He was also annoyed at the council's perceived lack of support for his business and his relationship with Petticoat Lane, commenting in the *East London Advertiser* in 1983:

> The borough council have supplied land for parking stalls at Chrisp Street market but Petticoat Lane. which brings in double the revenue, is the poor relation. We have done everything we can to please the local residents. We have put special rubber wheels on the stalls to make sure they don't make a noise but we just can't win.

Further disagreements with the council developed concerning the size of stalls, after the council changed the dimensions of the pitches that traders worked from in an attempt to modernise: the old pitch space, which dated to the Victorian period, was deemed no longer fit for purpose. These battles, too, continued for many years.

Most people, even those who visit the market on a regular basis, will not know Ivor Freeman. He is known only to those who work within the market. In fact, he describes himself as a 'public but private man'. Ivor has run a private market company called 'London Markets Corporation' for over thirty-five years and has had a stable of up to sixteen markets and 2,500 traders. Three of the markets are on private land off Brick Lane adjacent to Sclater Street and Cygnet Street, areas that were once previously bomb sites. He currently manages over 500 market traders and employs more than 100 staff. His company is run from a warehouse called 'Coppermill', also one of his private Sunday markets, on Dunbridge Street, at the edge of Brick Lane market.

It was at Coppermill that I arranged to meet this extremely busy man early one April morning in 2012. Although I knew Ivor well, as our paths regularly crossed over market issues, we have never talked in depth and so I was eager to hear the history of this intelligent, dignified, thoughtful but private entrepreneur. Ivor welcomed me with enthusiasm and wasted no time in telling me the story of the part his family have played in the history of Spitalfields, Petticoat Lane and Brick Lane.

Like those of so many other people in the East End, Ivor's family were originally from Poland. They came to the East End fleeing persecution and settled in the Spitalfields area. His grandfather was Solomon Isaacs, a shopkeeper and chairman of the Stepney Street Traders Association, who was instrumental in the campaign to allow Sunday trading. As Ivor explains:

> Because of the great Jewish trade Solomon negotiated Sunday trading instead of Saturday, which to this day is still in place in Petticoat Lane. The local authority in those days were men of honour and the traders were professional entrepreneurs and both mutually wanted the market to succeed.

Ivor's grandfather was also influential in helping many other family members to settle in London. During a time when opposition to further Jewish immigration was strong, he used his privileged business position and loopholes in the law to declare that he had 600 directors in his company, so freeing many from the pogroms in Poland. In consequence, his business was known as 'the foreign legion of Spitalfields'.

Ivor's uncle had a shop in Whitechapel opposite the Royal London Hospital. Ivor treasures a family photograph from 1916 of his uncle, driving a horse and cart, delivering a cheque for £500 to the British Red Cross for the war effort. He also sponsored a bed in the Royal London Hospital – this was well before the days of the NHS, when charitable impulses were essential to health care for the least affluent in society. He later transferred his business to Spitalfields and began a business in fruit importing, when he was known as the 'Banana King'.

Ivor's father and uncle carried on the fruit-importing business from a rented shop in Brushfield Street, Spitalfields, for over seventy years. Ivor recalls with great affection memories from a childhood spent in Spitalfields, where his life, from the outset, was about markets:

> I got to know all the traders and was extremely familiar with what they then called the 'East End Scene'. It was a safe environment but there were places where you didn't go, areas such as 'itchy park' … this is the park area next to Christ Church on Commercial Street – well, the park and … the church crypt was where the prostitutes, down and outs, the old seamen would go to sleep … It was a no-go area, but the area was part of what made the East End so vibrant. The other great influence was the docks; the East End was in full swing.

Ivor recalls as a boy of 15 being made to go to the fruit exchange in Spitalfields to learn the family business, where, he says, 'the whole area came to life with different auctioneers. They only had half-hour slots to sell their wares' but one auctioneer in particular, who auctioned half barrels of grapes, 'sold 30,000 half barrels in the half hour'.

His grandfather Solomon had a shop in Goulston Street selling material. 'The street was amazing. All the way up on both sides were stalls … selling chickens and the wives on the stalls would be busy plucking them. It was a unique sight.'

Ivor was keen to impress on me the importance of markets in the East End: '[There is] no doubt that markets were the backbone to the retail industry in the South of England, the likes of which will probably never be seen again, but is an important part of British history and should be protected and revered.' (I, of course, agree wholeheartedly with his sentiments.) From the markets, as he pointed out, came successful entrepreneurs such as Alan Sugar and Jack Cohen, the founder of Tesco. In the 1950s a stallholder called Mark Brafman, a dress auctioneer, used to cycle from Stamford Hill to his stall in Middlesex Street. He made his business so successful that when he died at over 100 years of age he left more than 500 shops called 'Mark One' to his son.

The exciting, vibrant world of markets obviously mesmerised Ivor. In fact, he said, 'I hear these days kids get a buzz from taking drugs but my buzz was from the markets.' Nevertheless, he took a slightly different tack from other family members, breaking away from the fruit-importing business and going into market management. It was at this point that he came to his beloved Brick Lane, which, he says, is still the most important area: 'Take the East End out of the man [and] there is no more man.' Ivor has run a successful business for nearly four decades and is still passionate about the markets, but recognises the changes that have taken place. As he saw it, in the 'golden age' of the markets the traders were different in character to those of today: all of them were entrepreneurs, and there was a respectful relationship with authority because businesses depended on it. Ivor believed that the traders of bygone years planned for a long future in trading, their main aim being to expand their business and leave it to their sons. I asked him what he thought had changed to the present day:

> The traders now have less respect because they have other safety valves for their income and so do not solely rely on the market for their survival ... The face of markets has changed, the resurgence of 1960s retro and the emergence of international cuisine ... I do not know [if it] is a fad or not, but the hard-core is the market. How long the trendy bits last is up to the trendies but markets will always have a future.

The buying public has also changed: 'People now come to meet friends, be entertained and get a bargain. The trader also has to be a sharp buyer as now you have to live off slim returns.'

In terms of a successful future for the markets, he believes that working in partnership is required between the private markets, the authority and the trader. He is at pains to be polite to me and respectful of the local authority, but is critical of its contemporary involvement:

The general consensus of opinion is that the local authority does not want markets and the new residents that come to live in the area want them removed, as if they would like the whole area gentrified. This would be a terrible mistake to let markets go as they are at the heart of the East End. Unfortunately the trader sees the authority as using bully-boy tactics and not giving [a] fair deal to the traders. In a modern world, why are there no toilet facilities [which he provides in his own markets], no meeting points for lost children, and why not let traders park their vans by their pitches for protection?

Ivor stresses that he deeply respects the market trader and is passionate about wanting to bring back more traders to the East End. 'The authority cannot ignore [the fact] that the backbone of east London are its markets, rich in history and people. Tourists still want to visit them in vast numbers.'

The thoughtful insights outlined above most probably are accurate inasmuch as the future of markets certainly depends on greater co-operation between trader, private enterprise and authority control.

Patter
How would one select items to buy or be persuaded to open up one's wallet in such a demanding and abundant market as Petticoat Lane? The answer lay in the Lane's other famous charm: trader patter. The patter and entertainment offered by various licence holders is now legendary; indeed, the Sunday market became, in essence, theatre. Traders took varying approaches to selling their wares: those who pulled in the crowds using patter were referred to as 'grafters', and those who did not were 'bunkers'. To attract a crowd was described as 'pulling an edge'. An example of a grafter *par excellence* was Lew Pickle, described in *Colour* magazine in 1972 as 'a rakish gentleman of middle age, his exotic features and darting eyes nearly concealed by his cloth cap. He is seen to be selling fruit and making more fuss about it than any of his colleagues.' He stated to the interviewer, 'I'm the only

man who has a licence at Scotland Yard to sell stolen property.'
Evidently, Lew Pickle was also known for appearing on television
in *The Bob Monkhouse Show*.

New Society reported several illuminating examples of
market patter in 1968. A trader in Middlesex Street known as
the Moulinex man (who sold kitchen gadgets) had a 'smooth
rapid-talking patter' always delivered in the same way. Picking up
a carrot and knife, he would say:

> Now ladies, how many times have you done this: one thick, one
> thin, one hump, one bump, one finger. Bleeding to death all day.
> Or use it with a cucumber. I know a lady in Blackpool who makes
> one cucumber last all summer. You never get indigestion that way.
> And you've got a machine by Moulinex, not by Tom, Dick or Harry.
> You've got a machine to last you a lifetime, not a daytime.

As he went on, the money would quickly change hands.

Sam Strong, who sold tea and dinner sets, won a contest in
The Hague for the best salesman's patter. He would stack a tea and
dinner service in one hand and begin his lines: 'The prettiest tea set
in the world, even the edge of the cups is gold – now, ten pounds
I could get for this lot, but I'm not asking that. Not even eight, not
seven, not even six or five pounds for the set.' Spotting a movement
in the crowd, he would continue: 'Hold your fiver, sir. Now I'll give
six of you the bargain of your lives … not five but three pounds ten
shillings for the sets that won the Solid Gold Cup!' But cnly one
hand reaches forward and Strong is left stranded. He reacts then:
'You greedy buggers …'

A trader selling blankets and sheets had a more mischievous
side: 'The price is ten pounds … the pair … I'm asking not eight.
Not six, not five but three pounds the pair … You married?' he asks
a girl at the front. She is. 'Marriage,' he says, 'is like the bank,
isn't it? You put it in and you take it out. Got any kids? No? On the
pill are you? No? Give her an instruction book, Fred. Now look at
these towels …'

Patter is less evident in the contemporary market, which is, in my opinion, the poorer for it. The practice exuded the excitement of the market and was a major part of the experience of Petticoat Lane, in particular. Although there is still much banter to be found it seems that 'patter' belongs to the market's golden age.

3

ASSOCIATED MARKETS

Although this book's focus is on what I deem to be the two most significant markets of the East End of London, its narrative would be incomplete without mentioning three other markets that interlink with Petticoat Lane and Brick Lane. Whitechapel, Bethnal Green Road and Columbia Road markets are connected to these larger markets not only by geographical proximity but also historically, in terms of the interconnecting families who have worked and continue to work each of the markets, some of whom work several of the markets on different days of the week.

It is part of a market's make-up for traders to vary their pitch and utilise the different localities at different times of the week. Many traders using the weekday markets of Bethnal Green and Whitechapel are supplementing their lucrative Sunday trade elsewhere. The histories of these smaller markets are tied in with benefactors and historical events, political unrest and local industry, and each has its own significant historical interest.

Whitechapel

'You cannot walk down Whitechapel without seeing suffering, drama and misery and it is unfortunate that I am drawn like a magnet to that place.'

Don McCullin, speaking in *The East End* (BBC4 series, London on Film)

The name Whitechapel derives from a church called St Mary Matfelon, which had whitewashed walls. This once stood on the plot of land that is now Altab Ali Park. The church was built in the fourteenth century and unfortunately was pulled down shortly after the Second World War, after suffering bomb damage. The surrounding fields, according to historical maps, indicated a windmill set in what is now the area of the East London Mosque. An ancient building that survives to this day is the premises of the Whitechapel Bell Foundry, which date to 1670; it is possibly now the oldest building in the area. The business here is over 500 years old and is famous for manufacturing Big Ben and the original Liberty Bell; it is still a functioning foundry to this day.

Inside the hall of the old Whitechapel Library, before it became part of the Whitechapel Gallery, was a tiled picture that depicted Whitechapel in 1778 as a local hay market. The market, though, is believed to go back as far as 1708. It is probable that hay was still being sold within the market until 1928, when the 'hay market' was abolished by an Act of Parliament. This part of the borough was still quite rural at that time, as evidenced by a drinking fountain and cattle trough by Commercial Road dated 1886. It is presumed that cattle were driven up Commercial Road to the slaughterhouses of the East End and to Smithfield market. Whitechapel Road, part of the modern A11, runs from the junction of Osborn Street/Brick Lane east to the junction of Cambridge Heath Road. The modern-day market runs from the junction of Vallance Road to the junction of Cambridge Heath Road and, until recently, held more than 120 market stall pitches.

As with Petticoat Lane and Brick Lane, with the influx of Jewish and other European immigrants in the nineteenth century the area soon developed its own bustling market. The scene is aptly described in a newspaper article from 1862 (www.mernick.org.uk):

> In Whitechapel Road, between the church and Mile-end Gate on this night everything is to be bought from the stalls which line the roadway, especially on the left-hand side going towards the Gate from the City. Amidst the flaming naphtha lights can be discerned toys, hatchets, crockery, carpets, oil-cloth, meat, fish, greens, second-hand boots, furniture, artificial flowers, &c. Round every stall are eager women, bartering with the salesmen.

The market of the Victorian era would have been as vivid as that of Petticoat Lane. The Royal London Hospital, set opposite the market, would have given the area in some respects quite a grand appearance, but its poverty always set Whitechapel apart. However, the area was alive with the typical entertainments of the day, such as vaudeville, theatre and other less savoury entertainments – and, of course, prostitution. Local entertainments and the Royal London Hospital come together, in fact, in one of Whitechapel's most famous stories: that of Joseph Merrick, also known as the Elephant Man. He was exhibited in a shop on Whitechapel Road and later rescued by Frederick Treves, a surgeon at the Royal London Hospital, where Merrick spent the rest of his life. He was not, however, the only curiosity to be found on that street, and reportage of the day describes a typical scene in Whitechapel:

> Every Saturday night there are many shows. Mysterious creatures exhibiting in enclosed square spaces about six feet each way. Hairy men, hairless dogs, gorillas, Aztecs, and giants. Beyond the Mile-end Gate the young English giant is located. By his own account he is 7 ft. 4 in. high, and has been presented to Queen Victoria and the Royal Family.

The market in Victorian times, although plainly home to some bizarre spectacles, in essence served the same role as did its neighbours: helping a struggling immigrant community to subsist. A familiar array of goods would have been on sale, including second-hand clothes, fruit and vegetables and fish and meat. But, with the entertainments on offer, it would probably have been a popular place, too, for family outings, children being enticed by a familiar cry of 'Okey Pokey' from the sellers of the popular penny sweets 'Hokey Pokeys', very sweet multi-layer ices as hard as a brick – a rare treat, perhaps, where every last penny would count.

Whitechapel was certainly one of the poorest areas of London and, alongside Petticoat Lane and Brick Lane, was home to a large dispossessed community. The market developed from its rural origins as a hay market, then, out of the need to find commodities cheaper than in the shops and as a way in which to scrape a living. The social problems experienced in Whitechapel were little different to those described for Petticoat Lane: poverty, slum housing and prostitution, to name but a few. Indeed, the Metropolitan Police in 1888 estimated that there were 1,200 prostitutes and sixty-two brothels in the area. Today, while the market thrives, the area is still beset with poverty, with a large number of homeless people, some of whom sleep rough, others in local homeless shelters. Many drug addicts and alcoholics are to be found around the market area, and theft and other anti-social behaviours inevitably follow. These are problems that have plagued the Whitechapel Road for over a century, and it is ironic that, despite advances in so many aspects of society, such issues are as prevalent today as a hundred years ago. In the middle of the market, opposite the Royal London Hospital, stands the drinking fountain erected in 1911 to commemorate the life of King Edward VII. The monument adjacent to this, erected in the same year by members of the local Jewish community, was originally cast in bronze, but was stolen so many times that eventually it was recast in a cheaper material. Only two years ago the pitches in Whitechapel were marked by brass plates, identifying the pitch numbers, but over a period of several months, under the cover of night, they were dug up one by one and stolen from the pitches. The traits from the past linger where impoverished communities remain.

The local council took over responsibility for running and licensing the market in 1965, and would go through regulatory struggles with its traders similar to those seen elsewhere. Like Petticoat Lane, the market was predominantly Jewish, but by the 1980s the area had many new immigrants, Bangladeshis being the largest ethnic population locally. The contemporary market reflects its local population's needs, with many Asian cultural dress stalls and Bangladeshi fruit and vegetable stalls that offer a staggering selection of vegetables, most of which are targeted at the local Asian community and are still completely unfamiliar to me. Exotic fish stalls, too, sell fantastic ingredients cheaper than most shops. Bangladeshis are by no means the only ethnic group represented on the market, however: other nation-alities include Iraqis, Turkish, Afghans, Somalians, Egyptians and Algerians. In more recent years waves of East Europeans from Romania, Bulgaria and Poland have joined this market of nations. The market still retains a handful of Jewish traders, some of whom have held licences on the market for nearly forty years.

The traders, like those elsewhere, are extremely hard-working. While the market is officially open from 8 a.m. to 6 p.m., the working day of the trader is far longer. The fruit and vegetable traders must be the most hardworking of all: they generally commence their day at 3 a.m., purchasing their stock from New Spitalfields market before arriving at Whitechapel market for 7 a.m. to set up their stalls, and do not leave until 7 p.m., when they have packed away their stalls and stock. It is these traders that are at the heart of the market, that pull the big crowds and create the atmosphere; their stalls are idiosyncratically Whitechapel. Although profit margins are slim, meaning that huge quantities of vegetables must be sold, there are good livings to be made – but at the cost of an extremely unrelenting lifestyle. Not only do a great number of the traders work the six days for which Whitechapel is licensed, but many also work on Sundays, making up some of the faces familiar in either Petticoat Lane and Brick Lane. The chance to earn more money in a different setting is obviously too enticing to pass up.

It is not surprising, with the intensity of the workload and stiff competition within the market, that occasionally tempers flare and arguments break out, occasionally escalating into fights; very occasionally, unfortunately, iron bars from the rigs have been known to be used as weapons in such brawls. I and other inspectors have had at one time or another had to break up fights and call for police assistance. However, these are far from the only pressures the market faces. Whitechapel's social problems frequently spill into the market, so that theft and anti-social behaviour are commonly encountered, as are drunks urinating or even defecating behind traders' stalls, drug addicts, beggars and young gangs attacking each other, and illegal fly-pitch traders selling illicit DVDs. These difficulties are enormous not only for the traders but also for the inspectors.

Although these images paint quite a depressing picture, they do not entirely reflect the day-to-day atmosphere of the market, which, although it has an intensity to it, is largely jovial and robust. The market is full of characters – not just the traders but also the hangers-on, those who like to immerse themselves in the market – and there are many strong bonds between individuals. Indeed, there are even good relations between traders and inspectors, who have spent years understanding the issues and problems that the traders face while keeping a well-enforced and regulated marketplace. Religious and political banter is often energetically engaged in, most interestingly and often amusingly, between some of the elder Jewish and Muslim statesmen of the market: such exchanges can often resemble rowdy debates at the UN. They usually spiral into racial abuse from both sides, but end in laughter, cups of tea bought and an uncomfortable arm round the opponent's shoulder.

Whitechapel's legacy is one of political and religious zeal, and it is no different today, as many different religious and political groups gather here to distribute their literature or preach their particular brand of faith. Muslim preachers and would-be converts, Socialist Workers Party activists and anarchists all vie for attention on the thoroughfare. One familiar character is a born-again evangelical Christian woman who stands outside the entrance to the Tube and waves her maracas about in one hand and a bible in the other.

The mixing of ethnic and religious communities here, however, does have its bleaker side, and extremist views are not uncommon. Asian stallholders who sell Bollywood-style DVDs have been attacked by zealots from their own communities because the covers of those DVDs show images of women in 'salacious' dress. In a similarly disturbing vein, there has been a resurgence of right-wing agitation from the English Defence League (EDL), a far-right group mimicking the cries of the National Front in a manner no less objectionable, nasty and dangerous. Members of this group had one or two minor clashes with local Asian males early in 2011, when the EDL were allegedly meeting in a public house, The Grave Maurice, in Whitechapel market.[3] Conflict between the EDL and the community of Whitechapel came to a head late in 2011 when a march by the EDL through Tower Hamlets and Whitechapel was met head-on by the local community, trades unions, the Labour Party and anti-fascist groups. In the end the EDL were largely dispersed after scuffles with police near Liverpool Street station. The market was on high alert, however, and patrols of market inspectors and THEOs were stepped up, keeping constant vigil over the market and the safety of those in the area.

---

3   The Grave Maurice is a pub that has stood on the market for more than 150 years; its name celebrates a Prince of Orange (the Graf Moritz) who helped the English defeat the Spanish in 1600. It would have been used as a stopping point for cattle drovers but later became famous as a pub frequented by the Krays and featuring as the sleeve art of an album by Morrissey. With such a history, it is a shame that the pub has now closed down and become a 'Paddy Power' betting shop.

While such organisations are threatening to community cohesion at large, intimidation from individuals can also be menacing, even if one understands the desperation of their circumstances.

Just as the problems of poverty and social deprivation are of long standing in Whitechapel, so too are many of the more market-orientated troubles. A particular annoyance was and is the use of the carriageway by traders, which has long been a thorn in the side of the market authorities. In the early twentieth century market traders were at conflict with the borough council, who deemed that traders were blocking the highway, and in 1928 the council took the decision not to renew licences in an attempt to close the market and rid themselves of a problem they felt was caused by the traders. Ten years later a judicial review against the council's decision was carried out, in the process of which it was remarked that the borough council at the time stated that carts and waggons occupied the carriageway and caused 'wastage of space and a great hindrance to the normal flow of traffic'. However, the review found in the market traders' favour, as it was decreed that there could be no evidence that their activities 'produce[d] undue interference and inconvenience to traffic'. Licences were renewed and the market has continued, but the arguments about road use have persisted. For the last twenty years various traders have sought to leave vehicles parked for exten- sive periods of time at the rear of pitches in loading bays along Whitechapel Road. The vehicles are often derelict and, as such, are both an eyesore and an annoyance to other road users. But in their own defence traders claim that parking their vehicles near to their pitches is vital to the safety of their stock and that parking spaces are so limited elsewhere that they do not have any other choices. It seems that some problems are perpetually recurring between traders and authority, but the Olympic project of 2012 may just be the decisive factor in resolving this issue.

Given the long-standing issues of Whitechapel's appearance and issues with anti-social behaviour, cleanliness and crime, it was considered a necessity in the light of London's hosting the

Olympics Games of 2012 that the market have an urgent overhaul. Tower Hamlets was one of the hosting boroughs of the 2012 games and, as Whitechapel was one of the main arteries to the Olympic site, funding was sought to clean up its appearance. Capital was secured for alterations to Whitechapel market that included a new stall design, resurfacing and improvements to include electrical hook-ups, lighting and waste control. In addition, a restoration project would restore buildings in Whitechapel to their former Victorian elegance. Unfortunately the plans did not meet with enthusiasm from traders, who complained that they would result in a protracted works schedule and smaller pitches and stalls. They also opposed the new design on the grounds of impracticality and long-term expense.

Traders and their representatives negotiated with the markets department, alongside other council agents, for a compromise on the proposed Whitechapel works. Eventually the council backed down and cancelled the new stalls for the market but the remaining work went ahead in the autumn of 2011. It remains to be seen how successful the refurbishments to Whitechapel market will be and how well they will be received by traders and

Whitechapel, 1905. (Courtesy of the Jewish Museum)

public, but this is yet another example of the tensions in the relationship between those who trade in the market and those who seek to regulate it: the trader believes that the market will become a shadow of its former robust self, while the authority strives for better control and a more sanitised space.

A visible and stunning success, however, was the restoration of the buildings opposite the Royal London Hospital. Restored and cleaned back to their original Victorian brickwork, they have a stunning impact upon the road. Their new face is a sizeable shift from what they had become and what at present still remains to the west: lost beauty covered by cheap and decaying paint, graffiti and neon signs advertising sari shops, fast food and immigration rights solicitors. Nevertheless, the restoration of the buildings has done nothing to quell the anger of the traders in Whitechapel, who have expressed their dissatisfaction at the 'improvement' works and other market issues by forming a shopkeepers' and

Whitechapel hay market, looking east, c.1926. (Courtesy of the Jewish Museum)

traders' alliance to make their collective view heard. They have held public meetings with Tower Hamlets' mayor Lutfur Rahman to discuss their issues, reflecting an increase in trader proactivity the likes of which has not been seen for a number of years.

Bethnal Green Road

The historical information on this particular street market in east London, which has quite obviously been overshadowed and dwarfed by its neighbours, is very slight. In fact, Bethnal Green Road is dominated by markets to the west in Petticoat Lane, to the north in Columbia Road and to the east in Roman Road. The market runs six days a week, excluding Sundays, and has approximately seventy pitches selling a range of household goods, ladies' wear and high-quality fruit and vegetables. Mike Munetsi's *A Guide to the Street Markets of London* refers to it as a 'shabby and a boring sight', which is, I think, an unfair summary; although the market does suffer from a lack of investment it is a functional and friendly place and has at one time or another been home to its fair share of personalities.

The origins of the market stem from an overflow of markets from the city in the early 1800s. It was enlarged in size when Brick Lane ceased to trade on weekdays. The market does not operate on a Sunday owing to a petition in 1833 from the parish church of St Matthew in Bethnal Green Road, who objected to the loud and unruly behaviour of the Sunday hordes. The market in its modern-day incarnation has been operating since 1853 and although Bethnal Green Road might not be considered a tourist destination it is an excellent example of a good local street market that has successfully fought off competition from supermarkets and other large shops. Yet it could also be argued, in this day and age, that the market survives not in spite of supermarket competition but because of the close proximity of such high street conveniences, which draw people into the area.

It does seem that Bethnal Green Road has seen busier times in the past, however, as an article in *East End Life* from April 1999 suggests. In it, well-known trader Pat Thorpe talks about its history. Pat, otherwise known as Perfume Pat, is a robust, loud, jovial and intelligent woman who epitomises the image of a market trader. She still trades to this day, selling highly desirable perfume not only in Bethnal Green Road but often in Brick Lane and Petticoat Lane. Pat commented that the market 'had a reputation for the finest fruit and vegetables in the area, especially from the Herbert family'. The Herbert family have a long legacy in the street markets of east London, with stalls once in Brick Lane (now sadly gone) and in Roman Road and Roman Road Square, but it is the Herbert family member who once traded in Bethnal Green Road, Peter, that I recollect the best.

Peter Herbert was a wry man with penetrating dark eyes. He always wore a flat cap from which wisps of black hair would protrude. His stall was always full of good-quality fruit and vegetables and hidden behind his cauliflowers every day there was a pint of beer, which he would furtively sip on during the course of the day. Peter was at odds with a changing market, often commenting 'the Turks are coming', elongating each word to emphasise the menace that he perceived the new traders represented. Although I did not share Peter's view of the world, he could certainly be entertaining. I later found out that Peter was the brother of the famous horror novelist James Herbert. The market certainly misses characters like Peter, but the quality fruit and vegetables remain, now sold by the Cucchis and Dearans, whose product is admired and purchased by professional chefs.

As Perfume Pat is one of the veteran traders on the market, serving in Bethnal Green Road and the Lanes for over thirty years, I was intrigued to know more about her personal history. And so, on a cold bright day in the autumn of 2011, I had a long, rewarding discussion with Pat, whom I have come to admire as a proud and immensely capable woman. Although at first sight she appears to epitomise the stereotype of the East End market trader, she is an intelligent, determined, honest and highly successful business-woman who has worked extremely hard to have a business that people come back to time and again. It is a matter of pride to her that she sells genuine perfume, which she imports from the USA.

We started our talk with the London riots, in which Bethnal Green Road was affected. Youths were seen in stand-offs with the police between the trader rigs facing the street, and video clips were posted on YouTube, but the events here were little reported in the mainstream media. I then learned, to my surprise, that Pat holds similar left-leaning views to myself and wishes that George Galloway was still MP for Bethnal Green: 'He was sympathetic to the traders and their parking issues.' Then Pat announces that George Galloway would have known her father's brother, who 'was a councillor, and not just a socialist councillor – he was a communist. [H]e came from the Gorbals of Glasgow extremely poor … [and had] never seen a joint of meat before he came to London. [He] got a job cleaning windows in Brick Lane before getting involved in politics.' Pat's father also held strong principals. Serving in the navy he was shipwrecked in the Indian Ocean and spent a long time in South Africa. He witnessed the beginnings of apartheid and was sickened by the treatment of the black population. After serving in the Second World War he was held captive by the Japanese, barely surviving, but none the less he held on to his humanitarian beliefs. I mention Tony Benn as my personal political idol, which meets with her approval, although her own soft spot is reserved for the late John Smith. Our talk reminds me of Tony Benn's comments in the *Daily Telegraph* (2009), that:

> politicians are divided into signposts and weathercocks … Margaret Thatcher was a signpost. The trouble was, I thought her sign pointed in the wrong direction. She was not affected by spin-doctors, she said what she meant and people knew what they were voting for. I see myself as being more of a signpost, like her.

Moving away from politics, Pat bemoans the state of Bethnal Green market; she is annoyed at the lack of progress towards improvement on the part of the council. She is also keen to point out rules that she feels disenfranchise traders, such as the new parking rules in Bethnal Green Road which mean that 'traders can only bring their van to their pitch after four'. In her role as trader representative she pointed out to the council: 'I'm self-employed, I can come and go as I please. I might have childcare issues – it's ridiculous … the council man on the phone started saying "you have made some valid points, maybe we can review at the next –" Don't give me that council speak … what a waste of time.' Pat has no time for bureaucracy and does not mince her words, but I am saddened that, for all her fighting talk, it seems that little has changed since the interview she gave to *East End Life* in 1999, where she called for some simple improvements to the market that could 'inject new life': 'we need more parking space around here to attract customers'. Wanting also to attract new young traders to the market, she had praised and celebrated the stallholder's life: 'a job on a stall is good teaching for the young. It teaches them discipline and hard work and how to deal with people. That's what the job's all about – dealing with people.'

Another trader who has been a presence on Bethnal Green market for many years and is now, perhaps, the elder statesman of the street is Norman Organ. Norman is a quiet and unassuming man

Perfume Pat, Bethnal Green Road. (Courtesy of Phil Maxwell)

of stocky build and with greying hair, who looks surprisingly fit for his 70 years: in fact, he looks the part of a man whose profession it is to sell fruit and vegetables. He is perhaps one of the last traders to use the old Victorian trolleys on wooden wheels, which is owned and maintained by a small local company operating out of a lock-up in Squirries Street. His stall has a good display of traditional 'English' fruit and vegetables which his loyal but ageing customers queue for on a daily basis. His trolley is adorned with the St George's flag, wafting gently in the wind and speaking of a bygone age.

Norman proudly spoke to me about his life on the market. Gathering an envelope from under his rig, he pulled out a photograph and said, 'These were my first three customers.' I looked down at the photograph to see the faces of the Kray brothers gazing back at me. 'Really?' I reply. Norman giggles. 'No, not really, but I did know them well; they always used to eat in Pellicci's café.' Then, with great pride, he shows me his original licence, dating from 1985, which he also keeps under his rig.

Norman was born and brought up in the area and has always been connected to the markets. Before he came to market trading he worked on the docks for twenty years, after which he helped his brother, who had a market stall in Bethnal Green selling flowers. He told me:

> I've always done fruit and veg and started on pitch number twelve – no one there now – but moved down to the pitch I'm on today. I've had good days out of it and I've had a few rag days but it's how you treat people. The best days are gone. Years ago you had more characters. One of the best stalls on the market was a guy called 'Leslie the meat man'. He only came out on Fridays and Saturdays but he had queues going all the way down the street. I remember once there was three creepy-looking characters eyeing up his stall and I thought I'd better go and warn Leslie, who was chatting with a friend in his car. When I went over to mention the blokes … I … saw he was ready with a big meat cleaver. I thought, my God, I'm not worried about Leslie – if they had any sense they'd be running by now.

Norman is one of few traders left who rise very early for the market and pack away mid-afternoon, in the traditional way, but there is no doubt that he has a loyal customer base and the market would be a lesser place without him. He is from a stock of hardened traders that withstand the cold and rain unsentimentally, his no-nonsense approach to work befitting the hard life of the market trader.

The market has undoubtedly seen many changes over the years and the ethnicity of the market is considerably more diverse than even fifteen or twenty years ago. As with Petticoat Lane and Brick Lane, it is now full of people from many different cultural and religious backgrounds, but even now it retains an air of the old East End and some of the divisions and opinions that were once common in this northern part of the borough still resonate quietly in the background. It is, nevertheless, a friendly market despite the traders' slight exasperation at the lack of development they would like to see for their marketplace, and one I enjoy visiting. Happily, it remains very much a local market, supplying necessary weekly household items to the local community. There is a character here that is worth appreciating, and one which can be enjoyed if one takes the time. Refurbishment and investment is required, however, if the market is to be relevant for future generations.

Although there is much to be said for this respectable local market, there are many other aspects of this part of the borough that deserve mention. The Museum of Childhood is nearby and the church of St John, which faces Bethnal Green Road, has been a presence since 1828. However, it is Pellicci's, an Italian-owned café, that is the most frequented establishment in Bethnal Green Road. Its fame lies partly in its Grade II listed premises, with its Art Deco-style interior. It still serves many market traders, alongside a growing number of bohemian artists and students. Only recently I saw Michael Gambon sitting outside the café enjoying an English breakfast and cup of coffee; we exchanged a rather surreal morning greeting. The other big draw is the Bethnal Green working men's club; as dark as the market is light, it plays to the outrageous and eccentric side of the area.

It is characterised by burlesque and contemporary music, by drag queens and young hedonists; its clientele spill out into the market arena after the doors close and the street begins its own theatre.

Columbia Road

The area known as Columbia Road was previously known as Nova Scotia Gardens, Birdcage Walk and Crabtree Lane, and once formed part of a droveway for livestock coming from Essex to Smithfield; this locale had been used as a rest area by drovers. By the eighteenth century locals would sell general goods alongside the cattle drove. This continued until around the mid-1800s. The area was also developed for clay for brick making, but when demand dwindled the district soon deteriorated and by the early 1800s, where brick clay had been extracted, the area was left barren and became a dumping ground for waste.

In 1830 Nova Scotia Gardens became a notorious area plagued by a gang of resurrectionists (bodysnatchers) known as the 'London Burkers' after 'Burke and Hare'. The gang stole freshly buried bodies to sell to medical schools, but came unstuck with the delivery of a 14-year-old boy whom, they eventually confessed, was not a fresh corpse but a drover on his way to Smithfield market that they had killed. There was much evidence, in fact, to suggest that the gang had committed multiple murders. They were arrested, tried and hanged but the public – and, indeed, the police – became fascinated with the case to such a degree that the police charged the public to see the bodysnatchers' house and sold souvenirs until nothing remained.

The area degenerated thereafter into an appalling slum, which inspired Angela Burdett-Coutts in 1869 to set up a school for ex-Spitalfield weavers and build a covered market in the Gothic style with the potential to hold over 400 stalls. The plan for the area was also to include cheap accommodation for traders and shops to surround the market. The area was rebranded 'Columbia Market Square'. The market's intention and driving force was to sell to the 'needy poor', and great efforts were made to sell nutritious products, including one of the main food items, fish, which was imported and traded from local east London ports. Indeed, the supply and trade of fish was so popular that the market was known for a short time as the Fish Market.

The plan for the market rested, however, on an extension to the railway route from Shoreditch directly into Columbia Market Square, but this plan met with many objections from the City of London and failed to materialise. Although at the beginning, as intimated above, the market flourished, it soon fell short of its objectives in other ways, as food supplies were not cheap and the poor thus failed to benefit from Burdett-Coutts' vision. Traders were also put off by the strict regulations enforced in the market; eventually they abandoned the building and returned to sell on the street. The area was rebranded to its now permanent status as Columbia Road.

The covered market closed in 1886 and was used as warehouses and workshops until its demolition in 1958. Only the wrought-iron railings of the original building remain today. Originally the market operated on Saturdays, but it moved to Sundays following demand from the local Jewish costermongers for an outlet for their left-over produce. It was, however, the French protestant Huguenot immigrants of Spitalfields, who had brought with them their love of flowers and birds, who would have the greatest influence on the market and set it on its present course as a flower market. The 'Birdcage' public house, at the western end of the market, is named for the legacy of birds on the market.

The market was highly successful until the Second World War, during which flowers were not sold to the public. The market did continue throughout the war, however, as traders switched to vegetables and fruit as a result of the government's 'Dig for Victory' campaign. The market was also bombed, causing major disruption, but at this time the warehouse space under the derelict market building fulfilled a new role as an air-raid shelter for residents and traders alike. It was not until the 1960s that the market again flourished, attracting the keen gardener and tourists.

In the late 1950s Tower Hamlets Council improved trader attendance across its markets by introducing and imposing 'a four week rule' that meant that traders would lose their licence if they did not trade at least once in four weeks, which was particularly helpful in developing Columbia Road. The increased attendance made Columbia Road a desirable market, attracting boutique shops and cafés and, of course, a wider range of exotic plants. The market's success, however, brought some problems of its own. An increase in trade meant larger lorries were needed to transport plants to the market, which in turn increased parking difficulty problems and noise issues for local residents. There was a campaign in 1992 to close the market, against which the traders formed an association, with long-standing trader George Gladwell as chairman. Alongside the council and local residents, the association sought to resolve the issues with better regulation and enforcement. After the market was saved it continued to grow in popularity, recently being voted the best market in London by *Time Out*. It continues to be a significant tourist attraction, with a stunning array of plants and flowers alongside a

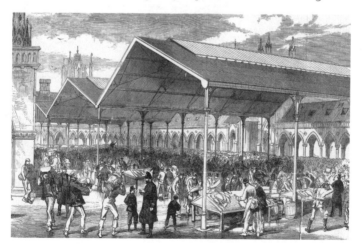

Columbia fish market, *c*.1880.
(Courtesy of Tower Hamlets Local History Library & Archives)

row of trendy boutique shops, and offers a perfect complement to Petticoat Lane and Brick Lane markets.

Columbia Road market would not be the place it is today, however, had it not been for one of the oldest traders on the market, George Gladwell. Born in 1929, George Gladwell is a formidable character who retains the strength and guile of a man many years younger. He is a constant presence on Sundays in Columbia Road as elder statesman and trader representative, a source of unparalleled knowledge and advice for public, traders and inspectors. But George is more than this: he is the architect of the market's success.

Columbia market, 1927. (Courtesy of Tower Hamlets Local History Library & Archives)

George Gladwell is used to being interviewed, as he is in constant demand for features on Columbia Road from gardening journals and television programmes worldwide. He was kind enough, however, to allow me to interview him at length concerning the history of Columbia Road and his personal history, which are, I quickly discover, completely entwined.

George was born and brought up in the countryside near Havering but encountered the city from an early age, when he would make a 20-mile journey to attend secondary school in Walthamstow. Being bright and ambitious, he graduated to architectural school but, not enjoying the 'office' life, he joined the army. With boyhood farming and mechanical experience to call on, he entered the Royal Electrical and Mechanical Engineers. George enjoyed his time in the army, rising through the ranks and serving in many countries of North Africa. When he left the army in 1949, not wishing to go back to architecture, he recalled the farming work he'd done and after some time rented a plant nursery. This was the pivotal point in George's life. He quickly showed entrepreneurial ingenuity, setting up a mail order service for seeds and sending cut flowers to Spitalfields market and Covent Garden. The flowers were packed up and sent on overnight trains to reach the markets fresh and in time for early trade. The work was, however, extremely hard: 'You had to work 14 hours seven days a week.' Encouragement from a market trader friend led George to become a trader in Romford market alongside his nursery work, and through another market friend, who had a pitch in Columbia Road and asked George for a lift there one day, he was introduced to his present market. George recalls: 'I had an old ambulance which I picked him up in, and stayed with him all morning but Columbia Road in the winter of 1949/50 was awful, I thought what a dead hole in the world this was.' But as the morning had worn on a few more traders joined them and a few people came to visit the market. After about three weeks George decided to stay on the market and managed to work for about six months free of charge, before an inspector came round to collect a few shillings for the pitch. Although the market was very much a seasonal one George enjoyed the life and excitement it offered, which contrasted greatly with the countryside life at home. The market manager at the time, Tim Castle, allowed George to 'inherit' two pitches vacated by a friend of his who had passed away.

'In the 1950s,' George explained, 'the council decided that they wanted to do something for the market and insisted that traders came out at least once every four weeks, which in the end encouraged me to come out every week.' As previously noted, the market benefited from this policy, and began to grow in popularity: '… and by the 1960s the market really opened up as lots of people wanted to trade there … there was a lot of profit to be made and of course the council got involved and the rents went up.' As the market grew in popularity it began to assume the identity that remains to this day, with many pitches run by close family networks.

It was George Gladwell's involvement with the market that has helped shape this success. With only a little modesty, George stated that he was 'responsible for the success of Columbia Road. In fact, it should be called Columbia Flower Market, as that's the title I gave for the promotion of the market when I started the mail orders and advertisement … in the 1960s, but the council insisted on it being called Columbia Road.' In fact, George really did catapult the market into the imagination of the public by advertising it in gardening magazines which led, in turn, to a good deal of film and television interest, including from *Gardener's World*; it even had its own series on BBC TV. This led to a noticeable increase in visitors to the market, with a measurable impact upon its continued success. Traders began to earn a lot of money but could not resist retaining the competitive edge and would, at times, still 'try and beat each other up trying to sell goods too cheaply'.

As far as the market's relationship with the local authority and its future are concerned, I was surprised to hear that George was in favour of proper regulations. 'Traders moan about the council regulations but they're better off with them; regulations can be changed but if there's too much confrontation the council won't change

George Gladwell. (Author's photo)

them.' The market's best times, according to George, were the late 1980s and 1990s, up to the economic slump of three years ago. At present he feels that the market is in 'limbo', and that it may be a good idea to lengthen the space it occupies, although that might also lead to more problems, such as difficulties with parking.

He recalls past days on the market fondly, remembering various characters: 'I remember a man we called the "the Rose guy" who would stand on a table selling roses … [and] would entertain the public by insulting them, saying he'd sort out their wives. The catcalling gives the market its atmosphere.' The inspectors in those days, unfortunately, had already discovered the benefits of the corruption that would follow in other places subsequently: 'There was one inspector who you had to give two bob for your pitch and two bob for himself but he got caught and was sent to prison; but amazingly, after being released, [he] would still come down the market trying to collect money.' There were also some dangerous moments on the market: 'A man once came at me with a knife as he thought I'd insulted his mother, but … I defended myself with a plant box until some other traders came to my help.'

George is justifiably proud of his achievements for the good of the market, but his involvement goes beyond those successes. In his role purely as a trader he was keen to tell me that his knowledge of plants was second to none, with many of his peers regularly sending their customers to George for advice on growing and planting. He is 'Mister Columbia Road' (or perhaps he would prefer 'Mister Columbia Flower Market'), and the market would not be the place it is today without his keen involvement and his dedication to its success, which have made it one of the most attractive markets in London. George tells me he still has many plans, including writing his autobiography, and mentions that his daughter might carry on with the business one day, but I know he is loath to give up the life and market that he is devoted to: 'I love the market, watching and listening to the public and traders. I even made a 5-minute film once, only of peoples' feet passing the stall. I thought it would be interesting – and the legs, of course,' he laughs.

4

BRICK
LANE

'Among the hidden things'

(From Dante's *Inferno*, Canto III)

'Real Objects, Real Stories' was the title of an exhibition of artefacts from the *Titanic* on display in London in early November 2010. It flickered before my eyes in the form of an advert on a double-decker bus while I was crossing Bethnal Green Road on my way to Brick Lane market one cold and drizzly morning.

But it was real objects of a different kind that fascinated me. I recalled then my first duties back in 1996 in Brick Lane market, which spread over an area covering Brick Lane, Cheshire Street, Sclater Street, Cygnet Street, Hare Marsh Street and Bacon Street. My colleague and I began our patrol in Cheshire Street, opposite the Repton Boys' Boxing Club, a fascinating building established by Repton Public School in a former Victorian bathhouse in 1884. Aside from our general duties, it was our task to discourage the illegal trading taking place in this area, which was located only a few yards from the edge of the legal street market.

> I was not prepared for the disorientating and bewildering scene that greeted me. A throng of people mingled and pressed together, all with

eyes fixed on the curious objects laid out on the ground – over the pavement, around trees, in any place where items could be displayed to entice the public into parting with their money. There must have been as many as thirty or forty traders in an area of street no longer than 100 yards long, with hundreds more people examining the items for sale. I looked down at these objects, as inquisitive as anyone else, and to my astonishment saw what could only be described as rubbish: one old black court shoe with a worn heel, a broken teapot, a pile of old, dirty, crumpled clothes, used undergarments, belt buckles, old radios, costume jewellery, batteries, bicycle parts, old LPs, an occasional small suitcase – masking its contents, porn videos – hammers, screwdrivers, plugs, nails and wires, unwanted children's toys. There was even one woman selling the Sunday morning newspapers, neatly laid out in title order, all selling at half the correct price, presumably stolen from outside a newsagent in the early hours of the morning. Even the cars lining the street had their boots open, displaying similarly odd assortments of eccentric goods. Interspersed among the 'junk' were boys on bicycles that, as my colleague pointed out, had probably been stolen the night before and were now to be redistributed to a new owner. 'Welcome,' he said, 'to the Thieves' Market!' – evidently, a term coined by the police for Brick Lane market. The scene was an Aladdin's cave from a parallel universe where all that did not glitter was apparently worth its weight in gold.

The appearance of the illegal traders reflected the eccentricity of their wares. There were young boys dressed in jeans, trainers and baseball caps, looking pallid, angry and aggressive. Older men were wrapped up warm in tired old casual trousers and jackets made from imitation leather. They represented a huge variety of ethnic backgrounds, as betrayed by their accents, and their expressions were redolent of their disillusionment with their lot. Furtive glances were made in our direction as they realised that we were there to call a halt to their activities. At that time Brick Lane was not the fashionable area that it is now: this was a market that the inspectors considered as the poor relation to Petticoat Lane – and,

Former flea market trader, Thomas Frederick Finch. (Author's photo)

Brick Lane market, 1988. (Courtesy of Phil Maxwell)

in a lot of ways, they were right. To my unseasoned eye on that day it resembled a scene out of Dickensian London, or a Hogarth engraving, reminiscent of Gin Lane or Beer Street. This was the beginning of my life as an inspector in Brick Lane.

Under the arches

I did not have to wait very long to discover that Brick Lane market was far more than the boundaries of the legal market. Later my colleague and I were reposted to the other main area of 'illegal' activity. This was at the top of Bethnal Green Road at the junction with Sclater Street and Wheeler Street. As we walked to our new positions through the crowded market I took in the sights and sounds of numerous loud and colourful traders selling a bewildering array of possessions, but there was no time to take all this in, as we had more pressing tasks elsewhere, dealing with those illegal traders who must be moved on and, if necessary, reported.

The scene was a mirror image from our encounter in Cheshire Street, except that here the dozens of traders lined the remains of the viaduct at the top of Bethnal Green Road, continuing around the corner into Wheeler Street and underneath the railway line, in what can only be described as one of the most ominous and intriguing parts of the markets of the East End. The remains of the Eastern Counties Railway Company's viaduct, built by John Braithwaite, all that is left over from the approach to the now-demolished Bishopsgate station, is home to a way of life far beyond its original purpose. The area was sanctuary to not only yet more illegal traders but also vagrants and prostitutes. On my first visit I felt like a naturalist entering a dark cave, the makeshift lighting system illuminating only small areas where it appeared that scurrilous deals of some sort were being undertaken, accompanied by shifty sideways glances, muffled voices and rustling bags. But I soon learned to shift my gaze from that of naturalist to anthropologist, as I needed to quickly digest the activity before me and to ascertain who were the illegal traders I was supposed to be moving on.

Historical background

Brick Lane's metropolitan history can be traced back as far as Roman times, when the area, which lay outside the city walls, was used as a burial site. One early such site was Lolesworth Fields in Spitalfields. This aspect of the area's history certainly establishes the idea of the area as liminal, set on the margins, outside society, and plants the seed of Brick Lane's often unsettling and nonconformist history.

Throughout the Middle Ages Brick Lane was a rural area characterised by elm trees and small-scale dairy farming. In the 1500s the brickearth deposits in the area were quarried for brick and tile manufacturing, an industry which was to change the direction and importance of a hitherto small and unremarkable street called Whitechapel Lane. It would now always be known as Brick Lane. The manufacturing of bricks and tiles would see the largest and most significant use of industrial methods of the time, but the development of Brick Lane and the brick manufactories under the Tudors was only the start of Brick Lane's varied and significant journey. The Old Truman Brewery is perhaps the most recognisable building in Brick Lane, a legacy of an industry that came to the area in the seventeenth century. In my opinion, it is as iconic as Norman Foster's 'Gherkin' or any of the other city skyscrapers. Although the brewery's chimney is dwarfed by its modern-day counterparts, its place in the skyline as a memorial to London's industrial past is no less significant than theirs. Within Brick Lane itself it is no less momentous in its role in marking the territory of the Lane, standing as it does full square at the centre of and, indeed, bridging the street. To its south lies the Bangladeshi community and to the north a predominantly 'white' community; and until 1965 this point marked the borough line between Stepney and Bethnal Green. In very recent times, it appears also to mark the limits of the gentrification of Brick Lane, contrasted against the more downmarket appearance offered by the old curry houses. The brewery, now hosting events and art exhibitions, is flanked by the area's markets: both the more recent trendy and vintage-style market and the historical street market.

In the seventeenth century a street market known as the Rag Fair began its life in Rosemary Lane (which later became Cable Street and the site of the famous anti-fascist demonstrations). The original area of the Rag Fair, which was opposite Whitechapel, eventually spread to Brick Lane. The development of Whitechapel, Brick Lane and surrounding areas, including Spitalfields, was particularly significant. By the mid-1700s the area was substantially developed and no longer resembled an industrial wasteland in which bricks were ferried by cart between field and brick kiln in Whitechapel. Small businesses and markets came hard on the heels of a growing immigrant population and the proliferation of manufacturing industries. As in other parts of the

East End, poverty and poor living conditions were rife: John Stow describes Brick Lane's housing as 'filthy cottages' and a rector of Christ Church described the area 'as a land of blood and beer'.

Its reputation as a lawless area, like Petticoat Lane's, was already growing, and, indeed, came to outstrip that of its fellow,

Brick Lane, 1895. (Courtesy of Tower Hamlets Local History Library & Archives)

Brick Lane looking north, early twentieth century.
(Courtesy of Tower Hamlets Local History Library & Archives)

being characterised by gangs and the handling of stolen goods.
Brick Lane, too, was attracting various immigrant communities,
including East European Jews and Irish. The most significant
immigration came in the years between 1880 and 1905, when
Brick Lane was the main area of the East End ghetto and was
almost totally inhabited by Russian and Polish Jews. At this time
the area was already being described in negative terms: from
very early in the area's growth newspaper reports reflect criminal
and underworld activity, while John Hollingshead described
the Whitechapel community in *Ragged London in 1861* in the
following terms: '… half of the residents are thieves, costermongers, stallkeepers, professional beggars, rag-dealers, brokers,
and small tradesmen.' Newspaper reports of the late nineteenth
and early twentieth centuries also indicate various forms of
lawlessness and unpleasant behaviour endemic in the quarter,
which ranged from theft to coin counterfeiting and animal cruelty.
The City Press reported in 1904 that a Brick Lane resident was
charged for obstructing with his barrow and spitting at a police
officer. The headline read 'A Dirty Fellow'. Charles Booth's

Brick Lane, 1920. (Courtesy of Tower Hamlets Local History Library & Archives)

survey of living conditions from 1888 to 1903 showed, in his *Descriptive Map of East End Poverty*, the area through which the viaduct passed as home largely to the very poor: many areas around Brick Lane denoted by the colours dark blue or black are described as 'Very poor, casual. Chronic want' or 'Lowest class. Vicious, semi-criminal'. Booth's team commented in their notebooks that various areas along the viaduct around Brick Lane and Pedley Street were home to thieves and prostitutes. The twentieth century would see a litany of controversy and bad press for Brick Lane, of which more later: but, regardless of the poor press the area has received, it is its shadowy, mysterious and frequently criminal reputation that has given the area a lasting legacy that fascinates visitors to the marketplace.

'A Thieves' Market'

I have already described my first encounter with Brick Lane, and my introduction to what was known as the 'Thieves' Market'. If there is anywhere in London that retains an atmosphere of distinct, dark menace it is certainly Brick Lane and its surrounding streets. The Whitechapel murders certainly cemented the reputation of the area as a dangerous and ungoverned place, but other types of crime also proliferated within the market and its surrounding streets. Petty crime, prostitution, theft and the activities of gangs and crime lords had a significant impact on the market's personality.

Like Petticoat Lane, the market of Brick Lane was a focus for the community. In a place of such deprivation it would be inevitable that the underbelly of society would show itself in the form of a variety of nefarious activities. Even to this day Brick Lane continues to be a focus of criminal activity, although with the recent gentrification of the area these problems are at last receding. It is, then, an odd paradox that Brick Lane has such great charm and that the market has been, and continues to be, so attractive to so many people throughout the years.

Poverty and the need to subsist in one of London's poorest areas are certainly instrumental in the character of the area. The 'chronic want' described by Charles Booth was certainly not in short supply in Brick Lane market, but a myriad of traders on the market and the thieves that abounded on the fringes of the Lane certainly attempted to meet that 'want', and enormous amounts of stolen and illicit goods would turn up for sale on the Sunday market. One should not romanticise the crime or the impact that crime had on the local community, but to understand the development of that Dickensian world, which still breathed its dark air to the end of the twentieth century, is to understand also the unique nature of the market. Our imaginings of the East End of the Victorian era are fuelled by the visions created by Gustav Dore or the writings of Dickens, which set the scene of a 'subterranean' London. Brick Lane in particular became a notorious example of that image.

Today the market is run by a great majority of honest and extremely hard-working traders, and the make-up of the market has many different facets, but its background is one of petty criminal activity and larceny that made it an alluring prospect to those trading in and exchanging stolen goods. Rogues found that they could peddle their stolen or counterfeit goods among the impoverished market traders and chancers, who were often recycling many times over the ragged unwanted clothes, bric-a-brac and other items in the hope of raising money for their families.

Problems with theft remain. Recently the area has seen an increase in the trade of stolen high-specification bicycles, probably as a result of growing gentrification, in which a large number of city workers who reside in the area have purchased very expensive bicycles as status symbols; and so a criminal element has crept in once more to feed off the rich pickings newly to be had. And, as described above, the market also has a number of illegal traders selling bric-a-brac and indeed anything you care to imagine, working along the arches in Bethnal Green Road and popping up in odd corners of the market; more recently, students supplementing their loans with a little illicit trading have tended to congregate along the now trendy walls of the Old Truman Brewery. Once again the authorities are battling to clear the market of its criminal elements.

A well-known character in Brick Lane, whom I had known for many years before I knew he was connected to the market, is Thomas Frederick Finch. I would occasionally exchange a few words with him in his favourite pub, the Brick Layers Arms in Shoreditch. Tom is now 70 years old and has the appearance of a person made eccentric by life's experiences. He is tall, thin and sinewy, with skin darkened olive in tone, but looks fit, is always lively and walks without stoop or impediment. He always wears a hat and his clothes and image befit the fashionable 'vintage' market in which he spends his time. At times, he seems distant, but you soon realise that he is sharp, determined and always aware of his circumstances. He has traded in Brick Lane as a legal trader but has also been a 'flea market' trader and on the cusp of illegality. Up to about a year ago Tom was certainly part of the 'new' traders that created part of the vintage revival of Brick Lane.

On a sunny day in March 2012 I bumped into him in Brick Lane outside the beigel shop, which has almost become his second home. He is often to be found here, sipping on a cup of tea and talking to friends. On that day he was playing a game of chess with a friend, the board resting on top of the waste bin, which provides the requisite elevation for a serious encounter. I bought Tom a cup of tea and asked him if he would be prepared to talk about his time on the market and as a flea market trader.

Tom said that I wasn't the first to ask him about his life but, nonetheless, told me his life story with enthusiasm:

> I was born when the Battle of Britain was going on, spitfires in the sky; my mother was a Gypsy who … you know … went out with the Yanks when they were over here. I was born and she couldn't cope so I was put in an orphanage. When I was 13 I left and joined the Merchant Navy. I went to the river Ganges where I was a Morse code operator [and] from that I went on and joined the Royal Navy, where I carried on doing my Morse code work. When the fishing wars were going on with Iceland in the seventies they sent me on the fishing boats to intercept Morse code. But it was difficult … it was so cold you couldn't send messages because everything was iced up. I had to climb the mast to the very top and chip away the ice. When I got back down I was deaf. [This, of course, explained the 'distance' that I sometimes observed in him.] Well, I left the navy; I sold my pension to the navy officer for £250 and with the money I bought a motorbike, the BSA 'super slash'.

His stories were fascinating, but I wanted to hear how he came to find himself trading in Brick Lane. Happily, he satisfied my curiosity:

> Well, I used to do all the building work round here. After I left the navy I was young and had a family to support so we used to go 'knicking' in people's houses and that and sell it on the market. You could get anything and because we sold it so cheap we always got rid of it really quickly. Of course I don't do that anymore but it was difficult; my wife was dying of cancer and I had four kids to feed …

Anyway, on the market I just sold anything I could, anything I knew people would buy, I always got my stuff for nothing. When you get older you slow down, your thinking changes … all my enthusiasms have gone. Now everything you get to sell, everybody's always got it. I used to sell from the back of my van but they stopped that, but it used to shelter me from the rain. It's a bugger in the rain.

Sensing that Tom wants to get back to his game of chess, I thanked him for his time, as his story is a valuable insight to the characters that have worked within Brick Lane on the fringes of the law – sometimes within it, but at times obviously outside it.

Characters, hard men and gangsters

The market is peppered with other unusual characters and eccentrics. One early newspaper report from *The City Press* in November 1869 alludes to the curious characters and bizarre sights and situations that are often found within Brick Lane in reporting the death of a man called Edward Daniels, who was killed by a tobacco pipe while in a local public house. 'The deceased, who was a cripple, was playing with a pipe when he fell down and the stem of the pipe stuck in his throat.'

More significant for the market than the intriguing person-alities, however, was the tough nature of people that worked the market, either legitimately or illicitly.

Charlie Burns is an extraordinary character and, much to my shame, I had not heard of him until Munir Ahmed, a market trader, suggested that I talk to him, as he was probably the oldest person on the market and would be able to tell me some inter-esting stories. When I asked Munir who Charlie was he chuckled and replied, 'Look, I'll introduce you and then later … you can to talk to him. He owns the lock-ups in Bacon Street and sits in his car all day checking what goes on. He must be at least 80 and he's spent his entire life on the market, so you must speak to him.' He took me around the corner into Bacon Street, where we found a battered old small blue Ford – that I must have walked past a thousand times before without paying much attention – parked alongside market pitches outside a warehouse.

Sitting inside the car is a very frail but alert old man; the years show on his gaunt face, the skin hollowing at the cheekbones, but his eyes are clear and he is receptive to our presence. Munir whispers to me, smiling: 'He doesn't like me very much so I won't hang around.' The introductions were made and I asked Charlie whether he would be willing to talk to me about his life on the market. I told him that I was a Toby as I had no wish to insult him, and it was possible that he would not want to speak to a council official, but my worries were unfounded. Charlie was polite, assuring me that he would speak to me on another occasion. His daughter Carol, who runs the business, stands by, proudly keeping an eye on her father; out of respect, I check with her that she is happy about my speaking to Charlie. She is equally friendly and charming, however, and so I am set for a fascinating encounter with one of the great Brick Lane characters.

A few days later I made my way to Bacon Street to see Charlie. As always, he was sitting in the nearside seat of his battered-looking car, sipping on a cup of tea, perhaps supplied by a member of his family or by one of the many who stop by to say hello to him. I'm taken aback by the level of respect and familiarity he seems to have with whoever passes by. Once more I sought Carol's approval to talk to him, but I need not have been so hesitant, as Charlie is easy-going and, despite his old age, is fully aware of what's going on around him, having exceptional hearing and eyesight. He beckoned for me to sit in the car with him.

I started by asking Charlie how old he is:

> I forget … 90 … born underneath the arches in Brick Lane, parents were paper merchants … you had your good times … you had your bad times …. I own four shops in Bacon Street and lived all my life in Bacon Street. The other day I was offered £350,000 for one of the shops but what am I going to do with the money? Go to Southend!

I remember the market: there was always a lot of foreign people selling potatoes, cabbage, fish and fruit ... [it] was Club Row for people like me, you picked up a living from the market. I sold paper to the city people when they visited the market; they couldn't help pass you and that's how you got your business.

I enquired a little further about Charlie and his family, and he told me that he had three children, including Carol. However, he was keen to keep talking about the market, a faraway look in his eyes as he reminisced. 'They were all heavy people. Do you know what I mean by that?' he asked me.

'No,' I replied.

'What I mean by that is that it was a tough world. They could look after themselves, but they also looked after other people as well. They were all nice people – hard as iron, but nice people.'

The best part of the market was the 'dog market', where they sold parrots, dogs, cats, mice, rats and so on. 'Rats?' I said, shuddering: they are a particular fear of mine. Charlie spelt it out for me. 'Yes, rats. R-A-T-S.'

It was a good market then, just before and after the war, before the mayor got rid of the animals. And he was the biggest animal of them all ... you had really poor people who slept under the arches – not like the homeless people now who want to be homeless. [And] when they got rid of the animals they got rid of the homeless as well.

In Bacon Street there used to be flats where a lot of famous people stayed to visit the market for a couple of days; everywhere you went there were characters. I remember meeting Ali and shaking his hand [I asked if he really meant Muhammad Ali]. Yes, ALI [rather irritated that I might think otherwise], he was fat, clothes couldn't fit him anymore.

On the strength of this story I asked if he liked boxing:

Oh yes, we brought the Repton Boxing Club to the market. I was president of the club for fifteen years. My brother, Tony Burns, is now the g'vnor of the club and has been knighted by the queen. People came from all over the world to our club – I say all over the world, I mean our country, 'cause that was our world. Though we went to France and Holland when things started opening up in the '60s. Those days we were all together. You didn't know the difference between black and white, everyone was poor and especially in boxing … [but] people were looked after; the poor never went without dinner and that's quite something.

Returning to the subject of the market, I wondered what the characters were like in his day. He replied, '[There were] a lot of Russians in those days. Everybody was a character. I remember a one-legged man selling fruit from a barrow … people used to try and trip him up … as he pushed his cart. They used to call him "sticky".' Charlie laughs:

This was a seven-day market but [it] became a Sunday market … the rest of the days moved to Bethnal Green. Also, there was a market selling more animals, even horses, cats, dogs and fleas, I think for experimental purposes. There was [a] character who used to sell racing tips … [There were] lots of characters on the market and famous people visiting – Liberace, Ali …

After reminiscing about his early life, telling me that he was a commando in the war, Charlie suddenly came bang up to date and announced that someone stole his lovely Merc. I asked him if he was going to buy a new car. 'No,' he replied. 'Too old, can't drive anymore …' As he appeared to be getting a little tired I decided to call it a day, and we agreed to talk another time. I thanked him, and then went to thank his daughter, Carol, who showed me into an extraordinary shed inside the lock-up where all the business affairs are conducted. Its walls were full of photographs of family and local history. Carol identifies a couple of photographs of Charlie and one with the owner of the beigel shop from the 1950s. Also on the wall is a picture of Charlie's brother Tony with the queen, confirming the story he had told earlier. I asked Carol how old Charlie is.

'Ninety-five,' she said. 'He got divorced at ninety-one!' The divorce was from his second wife; his first wife died when he was forty-six. Carol proudly shows me an old but pristine album of black and white photographs of his wife's funeral, with very touching and dramatic images of a traditional East End funeral procession coming through Brick Lane and Bacon Street. They conjured up a bygone age, as only old black and white photographs can. Carol went on to tell me that his ex-wife wanted £1.3 million from him, but didn't succeed in her aims. This was an indication of Charlie's wealth, but his obvious love for and ties with his family and his beloved Bacon Street and Brick Lane mean more to him than the money. She was just about to begin another story – 'You know Charlie also met the Pope –' when she was called away to attend to some business and I was left to wonder about this encounter.

A year later, in March 2012, again on a bright and warm day, I decided to go and visit Charlie once more, remembering that I needed to take a photograph of him and relishing the opportunity to hear more tales of his life and the market. I popped along to the usual haunt in Bacon Street. There was no sign of Charlie in his car alongside the lock-up, so I enquired inside. I was greeted by Charlie's son, who gave me the bad news that Charlie had passed away the previous week. He was 96 years old. His son was obviously deeply saddened by the loss, and I, although I had known Charlie only briefly, was also genuinely sad. I am grateful that we had a chance to meet, and I had been touched by his enthusiasm for life, his strength and his dignity. His passing marks the end of a long chapter in Brick Lane market's history.

Charlie was perhaps the oldest person connected with Brick Lane that I met, but the oldest trader, and the elder statesman of the market, is Ernest Bidder. In March 2011 I took the opportunity to talk to Mr Bidder. He has had a pitch selling fruit and vegetables on the junction of Brick Lane and Cheshire Street for more than half a century. Mr Bidder is a quiet, unassuming man who conducts his business without fuss or fanfare; as a result, I have had few encounters with him in my role as market inspector and so, consequently, I was eager to discover more about the man and his experiences in Brick Lane market.

Mr Bidder began by telling me that he was 64 years of age and had been trading on the market since he was 12. His father was on the market for ten years before that, so he was, perhaps, destined for a life on the market. 'I was born in Granby Street, around the corner from Bacon Street,' he said. His family initially had to fight to establish themselves on the market; because the Sunday trading laws only seemed to benefit the Jewish traders it was, for a long time, an enormous struggle to get an all-important pitch:

> When I started the market was sewn up by the Jewish traders. At first you could only get a licence Monday to Saturday, but that was useless, as it was a 'Sunday market'; but eventually, after a lot of struggle, we got a licence on the very pitch I'm on now. A nice inspector called Timmy Castle gave my father the pitch because he figured he'd suffered enough.

Mr Bidder tells the story without malice or regret, however. In fact, he is most gracious about all nationalities and races and saw the hardship of life as a battle that they all faced together.

Like Charlie Burns, he surprised and entertained me with his views on the conditions in the market and some of the characters that he has encountered:

> Rent was two shillings a week when I was 12 and the market was very good then, especially the dog market. The animals and birds were bid for under the hammer. Brick Lane was a very attractive market in those days. I saw a lot of film and television stars coming down the market; they couldn't resist the attraction of the Lane. I saw Tommy Cooper, Barbara Windsor, Sterling Moss and, about twenty years ago, Davina McCall. She asked me out –

'Davina McCall?' I ask, doing a double take. 'Do you mean the woman off the television programme *Big Brother*?'

Oh well, it was before she was famous like she is now. She was doing a bit of filming on the market and I caught her eye. She saw me working very fast. See, I could do a quadrupler when I was younger [serving four customers at once]. My brain worked like a fast computer, I could do all the calculations at once.

Although I was very impressed, I didn't ask if he ever did date Davina. But presumably he turned her down, as she did not appear in any of his other anecdotes.

Mr Bidder recalled the way the market used to look. There were a lot of Jewish shops and stalls. The shop opposite Mr Bidder's stall, now called 'Bashirs' and owned by market trader Munir Ahmed, was a pub, and the Moroccan café behind his stall was owned by a Canadian, although he couldn't remember what it was originally. He did remember, however, that the market was largely Jewish in flavour. He commented: 'When war broke out my father said that all the Jews ran from their stalls ... left all their goods and money ... as [they] thought they were going to get bombed, such was the fear ... they thought that they were personally getting attacked.'

I asked, a little provocatively, if he thought the market was better when he was younger. 'Well, the supermarkets killed a lot of business when they opened on Sundays. Our takings were affected within a month. So in a lot of respects they were better, 'cause we had all the trade people come here if they needed things on a Sunday.'

Slightly nervous of what I might hear, I then asked him about his dealings with my predecessors. He said:

Well they're a lot better now than they were then. I remember a guy in fifty-six or fifty-seven: he was horrible; he gave trouble to all the stallholders and made their lives a misery. He gave summons to loads of traders but thankfully he eventually got a job in St Albans ... Everyone was so pleased to see the back of him. A trader I knew who sold yams on the corner cried with joy when he left.

Mr Bidder went on:

> I had one bad experience with the council when I tried to work
> Whitechapel market when I was 18 or 19. I 'sub-let' a pitch Monday
> to Friday but Johnny Ambrose, one of the chief inspectors, caught
> me and did me for unlicensed street trading. It made life very difficult
> but I didn't do anything illegal after that.

Wanting, after that, to lighten the conversation, I asked him
to recount his experiences of those personalities who made
Brick Lane a more vibrant and interesting place, and he at once
brought up Prince Monolulu, already described: '[he was] one of
the biggest characters … he would walk through the market with
the feathers in his hat selling tickets for racing tips, a bit like what
the papers do now, but he sold them. [He] would sell them on
the 'bomb site' near Bacon Street, which they're developing now.'[4]
He went on:

> There was Jack, who would have a parrot on his shoulder and sell
> corn, and a trader called Stevie Howard sold bananas underneath
> the railway arches … once came to the market by hiring two cabs
> 'cause he didn't have a van or a car. Anyway, when Prince Monolulu
> died he took over the tipping game, I remember he would cut old
> newspapers to the size of bank notes then wrap a £20 note round
> them. This was to give the impression that he was flush or loaded,
> so punters thought he didn't need the money. [I] also remember a
> Jewish trader selling rolled herrings and other fish. He was stone deaf,
> all his customers had to write down what they wanted.

---

4   By this, he meant a local brownfield site on which a development of smart
    new apartments is soon to be completed. Prohibitive in price, they will
    undoubtedly attract wealthy city workers who, although they flock to the area
    for its attractions, including the street markets, often bemoan the market's
    presence when they move in.

Mr Bidder was quite obviously proud of his father and of his own honesty, determination and hard work. He remembered one occasion on which:

> My father once saw eight wallets by his stall [presumably the results of someone's pickpocketing] and said, 'Whoever put these here gets rid of them now, I'm trying to make a straight living.' My father was called Ginger. A bit like me. People used to say to him, 'You'll never be skint with that son you've got with you.'
>
> [The] market was a hard life though, you would take ladies out on a Saturday night and always have to work Sunday ... very difficult for a young man. I remember once witnessing two men trying to saw a man's arm off. Don't know who it was or what happened but [I was] shocked at the sight.
>
> I remember a shop in Brick Lane about fifty years ago owned by two brothers that burnt down, the brothers got out but one went back in to get something, maybe money, and burnt to death.

Mr Bidder told me this story in a very matter-of-fact way; although he remembered the tragedy clearly and must have been deeply affected by it, he accepted that life on the market was demanding. Poverty and hardship forced people into making uncomfortable or, indeed, at times fatal decisions. At other times, even the saddest of situations might contain an element of humour: Mr Bidder recounted the following of a fellow trader: '... a character called Johnny Bananas who sold bananas all his life; shortly before he died he went yellow. Not because of the bananas but [because] of liver disease.'

Mr Bidder's own life held as much interest for me as his tales of the market. He had early achievements in the boxing world and, as a result, connections with perhaps the East End's most notorious gangsters, the Krays:

> See, I was amateur boxing champion in 1964 and I represented England three times. Reggie Kray said to my father 'Your boy done well. Give him our congratulations'. My uncle used to take

Violet Kray [the Kray brothers' mother] out before she was married,
so that was the connection between us.

I asked Mr Bidder about the Krays and if he was impressed by
their boxing. He was a little reticent, saying: 'The Krays could
box a little. Used to train at the Repton Boxing Club when it was
in Bethnal Green Road. Charlie Kray used to drink too much.
[I] remember visiting Violet and seeing the boys; they looked
like butter wouldn't melt in their mouth. But then one morning,
about 5 a.m. [I] heard gunshots go off from the Carpenters Arms.
That's when Ginger Marks got shot.' This story, too, was told as
a matter of inconsequential fact; it was simply part of his life.
He wrapped things up by telling me that he now lives the quiet
life in Clacton. 'Took the opportunity when Thatcher privatised
the council homes: bought, sold up and moved out, but I still love
Brick Lane.'

Mr Bidder is another singular individual who has made a
lasting impression on me as a quiet and dignified person for whom
Brick Lane has been his life. Ernest and Charlie both represent
an older generation of the market who knew an existence characterised by poverty, but one which bonded people together. These
were men who made the reputation of the East End, the men
who gave the area its no-nonsense, salt-of-the-earth reputation.

But both of these men alluded to a far murkier side to
Brick Lane and its market. With poverty came, as always, crime,
with many unscrupulous characters out to exploit the vulner-
ability of Brick Lane and its inhabitants. All those in the local
community – the public, the traders and the faintly disreputable –
were subject to the activities of gangs and gangsters. Many of
the legendary gangsters of the East End were closely associated
with the market, either through their exploitation of traders or
punters, or because the market was within the territory of their
gang. As previously described, Jack Spot ran a racket 'protecting'
Jewish shopkeepers and traders from the 'blackshirts' in the 1930s.
He may have had some credibility attached to his name by his

actions in fighting fascists in Cable Street, but his protection racket was simply crime born out of depravation, poverty and a fight to survive in one of the most disadvantaged areas of London. Jack Spot was, unfortunately, by no means the first to exploit the area's circumstances and neither would he be its last.

Street artist Ben in front of his portrait of Charlie Burns. (Author's photo)

Mr Bidder, Brick Lane, 2011. (Author's photo)

Jack Spot's predecessor was the less well-known Arthur Harding, who was born in 1886. We know of him through his 'autobiography', entitled *My Apprenticeship to Crime*. Although this book is a revealing document about his criminal exploits, the justice system and his childhood, it is also incomparable in revealing the uncompromising and unsentimental nature of life within Brick Lane market from the end of the nineteenth century through to the first half of the twentieth century.

Arthur Harding was described by the police in 1908 as 'The king of Brick Lane' and was well known as a dangerous and 'slippery' leader of thieves, known collectively as 'The Vendettas'. He was as closely connected to Brick Lane as can be imagined, being born and brought up in Bacon Street and latterly in Gosset Street, off Brick Lane; it was no wonder that the marketplace would provide the opportunity to escape from an impoverished background, albeit in a less than usually law-abiding manner.

Arthur recalls Brick Lane as being 'a hotbed of vice, every kind of villainy could be found in the district and under the railway arches down-and-outs slept covered with sheets of newspaper'. There were many gangs ready to exploit whatever opportunities could be found on the edge of the poverty-stricken 'Old Nichol' area. The extreme poverty of this area and the enormous health issues that went with it must be remembered, and crime must have seemed for some the only possible way of survival. Evidently gangs congregated in a coffee house called 'Clarks', which was situated opposite Hare Marsh Street off Cheshire Street. Although Arthur had attempted to obtain work in various trades and had enlisted for the army it would not be long before he involved himself with the illicit activity of these gangs.

By the age of 14 Arthur was selling 'penny' toys in and around Petticoat Lane and, in particular, on the corner of Middlesex Street and in the public house The Dirty Dicks. The Dirty Dicks' correct name, according to Harding, was The Jerusalem Tavern, an obvious reference to the large Jewish immigrant population, members of which must have frequented the establishment. The pub was also home to various insalubrious activities, including prostitution, as Arthur noted: 'Many ladies of the town made it their rendezvous.' The pub was an obvious trading place for the sale of goods, stolen or otherwise. And for the next twenty years Arthur Harding would find himself in and out of prison and practicing his 'apprenticeship of crime' on the streets surrounding Brick Lane market. Criminal gangs specialised in different crimes according to the area in which they operated, and in the areas between Shoreditch and Hoxton the gangs were notorious for pickpocketing, counterfeiting and pimping. Arthur Harding even refers to Dickens' Fagan character as helping to show them the best methods of picking pockets.

Brick Lane was a constant presence throughout Arthur's life and he would have been familiar with the traders and the market environment. His memoir gives a flavour of the atmosphere at the time, in particular in Club Row, where you could buy 'a bird, canary or even a monkey. There is a bird market and a bicycle market. In fact you could find anything you wanted in one of the market streets.' His sister Harriet was a stallholder in Brick Lane and Roman Road markets and was also a friend of Jim Kray, the grandfather of the yet unborn and future 'kings' of Brick Lane, the Kray twins. It was in this familiar environment that Arthur seized his chances, soon finding an opportunity for theft when witnessing a gambling game in Bacon Street called 'pieman', where he stole a watch from a boy engrossed in the game.

Being involved in criminal pursuits, Arthur was well aware of policemen within the market area, often seeing them in plain clothes trying to catch the pickpockets; indeed, he was arrested for pickpocketing by a plainclothes policeman. He was now gaining a criminal reputation, becoming one of the 'dead end kids of Brick Lane'. However, he did not acquire his reputation for violence until he took revenge on two local gangsters who had assaulted his mother while he'd been away in Borstal. Putting an end to their reign of terror ironically propelled Arthur into gang life, and he began his thieving and counterfeiting career in earnest. In the early 1900s some of his most common victims were foreign seamen visiting the market and its surrounding area. Targeted for the large sums of money they tended to carry, they would be lured by 'ladies' and the gang would rob them, usually incapacitating them by garrotting them until they passed out.

Arthur Harding would exert a hold over Brick Lane for the next
twenty years, running protection rackets among the stallholders
and street bookies. He was also involved with the infamous
'Vendetta Affair' in 1911. This was essentially a pub brawl, but with
extreme violence, including the use of firearms, was employed
and a great number of people injured. Arthur was convicted for his
part in this incident and sentenced to a prison term of five years,
which ultimately put an end to his violent criminal activities.

Arthur Harding was 30 when he was released from prison and
once again found himself back in Brick Lane. He married a
local girl and began a new profession of 'hawking' in the market.
At the beginning of his 'apprenticeship' into market trading he
was shown the art of selling by talented Jewish traders, and it was
in Brick Lane, his home, that he would ply his trade: 'The old
clothes market was in the north part of Brick Lane; this market
was only held on a Sunday morning up to 1 p.m., when all stalls
had to be closed away.' The stalls were licensed for the cost of 'two
shillings a week', but a shortage of vacant stalls meant that Arthur
found it very hard to get a licence. As with many other potential
traders, this did not put him off and 'I would take a chance to
sell without a licence'. However, this proved unsuitable, as he was
always being moved on by the police, but, not shirking a challenge, Arthur appealed to the then local Liberal MP Percy Harris
and explained his predicament. The outcome of his boldness was
the granting of a licence, of which he was very proud, since he
was able to show his licence card to policemen, thus proving his
'honesty'. At last Arthur had come full circle, now plying an honest
trade within the market rather than using it as an arena within
which to steal, con or threaten people.

Arthur, although reputed to have held right-wing views and
been friendly with Mosley's blackshirts, condemned the 'vile'
abuse that Jewish people suffered. Although a strike-breaker in
1926 he was not immune or indeed cold to the struggle of the poor
who frequented and lived around the streets of Brick Lane. Indeed,
he was a witness to their poverty on a daily basis: 'If you were to

visit the old clothes market on a Sunday morning and see the vast number of people sorting out the piles of clothes, you would be surprised at the poverty of some of these people.' During the Second World War market trade was still very profitable, particularly in second-hand clothes. Many men had lost their lives in the war and widows made money selling their husbands' garments. Arthur maximised the potential to his business in second-hand clothes, reputedly buying up items from rich men in return for stolen ration books, which he had in turn bought from thieves.

Like so many other commentators on the East End, Arthur describes the huge ethnic diversity and types of trade in Brick Lane:

> You will find a motley collection of Irish, West Indian, Pakistanis, Indians, Maltese and other African Commonwealth citizens, all to be found on Cheshire Street on Sunday. The Asiatic people are the buyers of men's suits, sewing machines, preferably 'Singers', and even antiques for the African market, which are shipped out. Women come looking for cheap dresses, children's clothes, boots and shoes.

Arthur Harding continued to trade in Brick Lane and even bought a shop at 250 Brick Lane, but in his autobiography he has left a legacy for the market that perhaps he was not fully aware of. In particular, he made what is one of the most resonant comments about the condition of the market and its local residents when he said, 'Whatever the race or colour of their skin … poverty knows no barriers or caste distinction.'

The 1950s in the East End of London was an era just as savage as that preceding the war. The area had lost the benefactors that had once flocked there in an attempt to reform and improve the 'lot' of the East End communities. While the progressive Labour administration of the previous Mayor of Stepney, the then prime minister Clement Attlee, set itself to reform, tackling poverty and creating a national health service for the nation, the East End still languished in slum conditions. With the retreat of the benefactors there was a distinct power vacuum and the area was ripe for further criminal exploitation. And with the examples of Arthur Harding and Jack Spot in mind, the two most famous of East End gangsters, the Kray twins, stepped up to the mark.

I do not wish to repeat a history that is so familiar and well told elsewhere, but it is worth considering the background of these gangsters in relation to Brick Lane market. The Krays were familiar with the market and trod its streets, and the traders were familiar with the twins, who had been born and bred in the area. There is no evidence to suggest that they exploited traders, as their sights were set higher than the morsels that traders would provide; it is more significant, perhaps, that they were of the same stock as the traders: hard men who fought for a name, notoriety and riches. Although cut from the same cloth, these men spurned the hard struggle of market life and, indeed, the honour of the trader; but, nonetheless, they were engrained into the fabric of the area.

The Kray brothers were brought up in Vallance Road, a stone's throw from Cheshire Street. They boxed in the Repton boys' club and, later, drank in their favourite public house, the Carpenters Arms, which sits on the edge of the market. Boxing gloves hung behind the bar, which, it is rumoured, was made from coffin lids. The pub's notorious connection with the Krays goes beyond a pair of boxing gloves: it was outside this pub that Ginger Marks, a small haulage operator, was murdered in 1964, as mentioned by Mr Bidder, who heard gunshots go off on that particular night. The *Sunday Times* reported in January 1964:

It was about 30 minutes after midnight last Saturday when Marks, a smartly dressed man with red hair, freckles and horn-rimmed glasses, was walking past the Carpenters Arms pub in Cheshire Street. He stopped on hearing his name called from the darkness of an alleyway and turned to face a group of men.

Seconds later, there was a series of shots. One bullet hit Marks in the stomach. Before he fell to the pavement, other shots followed, one ricocheting off a 5ft wall behind him, and another entering his head at close range.

The reasons for this murder were not known for a long time, but it now seems that Freddie Foreman, a gangster who worked for the Krays, had a personal vendetta against Ginger Marks. Having been acquitted for the murder in 1975, he later confessed to the killing in 2000. The associations do not end there, however, for in 1967 a villain and hardman associate of the Krays, 'Jack the Hat', was causing the twins a nuisance by becoming uncontrollable and being persistently rude and arrogant towards friends and business partners. He had to be 'dealt with', and in due course was killed by the twins. It was in the Carpenters Arms that this plot was hatched.

Many years later, after the turbulent years of race hatred directed at the recently arrived Bangladeshi community and the fight against fascism in the 1970s and '80s, new gangs started to reflect the dominant ethnicity of the local community. As had probably been the case for all previous generations, gangs began as attempts to defend the local communities from which they sprang, and it was no different for the Bangladeshi population, where it was perceived that racial prejudice formed the greatest threat to the gangs' communities. The rise of gangs such as the 'Brick Lane massif', however, soon created an opportunity to turn 'protection' into criminal and violent activity for their own benefit. Nevertheless, the dominance seen by gangsters such as the Krays has yet to be repeated in quite the same way.

Club Row

'Colour and music in a grim landscape'

– from a newspaper article, source unknown

Club Row was the 'engine' of Brick Lane market. In fact, Club Row, known also at various times as the 'bird mart' and later the 'dog market', *was* the market. The market, which originally started in Club Row, quickly spread to Sclater Street, one of the three main arteries of Brick Lane market. The area in which the market took hold was at the junction of Sclater Street with Bethnal Green Road, against the backdrop of the viaduct arches that were already home to 'huskers', vagrants, hustlers and other street traders. The area must have been vivid with sound and colour, akin perhaps to a medieval fair, and the like of which we may never witness again in this country.

Club Row's origins date back to at least 1840, with roots in the legacy of the French Huguenot silk weavers, who had a penchant for small singing birds and a love of flowers, as noted previously. The birds brought 'colour and music in a grim landscape' of small dark sweatshops, and a growing public demand for them led to a developing trade.

In the latter part of the nineteenth century Club Row was at the heart of the east London ghetto and came to the attention of social observers. John Galt, a Scottish missionary who settled in London and was attached to the Tent Street mission in Bethnal Green Road, was appalled by the living conditions of the East End poor and photographed areas such as Little Collingwood Street, where, according to Charles Booth, costers, fish curers and thieves lived. Galt also took some extraordinary photographs of Victorian-period Club Row. His photographs, of course, also illuminated the work of his mission in the area and illustrate the importance and popularity of the Club Row market.

The demand for singing birds was enormous, and rich and poor alike flocked to the area. Traders and visitors were crammed into a relatively short and narrow street. In 1895 the *New Budget* magazine noted their popularity in an article entitled 'Down east on Sunday among the birds and bird-fanciers', which described the outlandish spectacle: 'From all the walls are hung wicker and fancy cages, and every cage has its inmate: a chaffinch, canary, bullfinch, starling or linnet.' The birds, being highly sought-after items, the fashion of the day, made a lot of money for the traders. Particularly popular were birds that produced a high number of 'julks' – a term given to the change of trill in a bird's song. The same magazine reports that a trader claimed that he saw thirteen gold sovereigns paid for a

chaffinch that could achieve ten julks. As the average middle-class
income at the time was approximately £200 a year, the price of the
chaffinch was easily a month's wages. While the trader's claims are
likely to be an exaggeration, in order to encourage higher-priced
sales, it does suggest the high value of songbirds at the time. Other
less desirable birds, were, of course, sold at more reasonable
rates to the common man – three shillings, for example, for a
'real Norwich cock'. The traders' banter and bartering was certainly
part of the atmosphere, as the *New Budget* reported when describing
a sale of a bird: "'Don't yer get a bringin' me any of yer one and
sixpence for a real Norwich Cock. If yer do I'll tell yer to go and
spend 'em at a bloomin coffee shop, selp me if I don't." (Roars of
laughter from the crowd.) "Three shillings or nothin's my price".'
The trader goes on to promise that the bird will wake the customer
up every morning for breakfast and gives his word of honour that the
purchase will be a happy and satisfactory one.

The *New Budget* article goes on to describe the practice of
'singing matches', where contests would be set up, generally in a
coffee tavern or public house. 'The cages of two birds would be
hung on a wall and uncovered at the same moment. The owners
have to stand in the gutter, watch the performance and score
the points from a distance.' The spectacle would be watched
in silence, with fair play being observed. Victory was awarded
to the bird who accomplished the greatest number of 'julks'.
The breeders and owners of these birds were well respected and
the practice became an institution in the East End as much as
pigeon-racing or bulldog fights did in the Black Country.

Club Row market also sold poultry, which would often be
slaughtered on the spot. However, the area quickly developed
into a more general pet market, where it was reported that even
exotic and expensive animals such as lions, tigers and racehorses
could be bought. Also on sale were creatures such as fish, weasels,
mice and, as Charlie Burns recollected, R-A-T-S, but the most
important aspect of the pet market by the 1950s was the sale
of puppies and kittens. At around the same time the market's

colloquial name changed from the 'bird mart' to the 'dog market', while the sale of other items developed, some ancillary to its main purpose, such as fish food and bird seed, but others more general in nature, such as fresh fruit and vegetables, shellfish, jellied eels and bicycles, the sale of which still continues today.

The 'dog market' was certainly enjoyed by thousands of people, and traders who can still remember it speak of it with great fondness and sadness at its demise. It was the subject of a sympathetic portrayal by a Miss E.M. Evors in a magazine article from *The Graphic* in May 1920, in which she describes the congested area of Sclater Street: '... the yapping and muzzled animals, the expert traders and patter and the discerning eye of the customers as they examine a dog before their purchases.' Some traders would buy cheaply in the dog market, only to sell later for twice the price in the West End to wealthier customers:

> On all sides you see toy-dogs, pets of the boudoir, poms and Pekinese, with cunning little faces. Nicely groomed and pranked out in pink and blue tie-ups like babies, they are fascinating scraps. Shy, shivering little creatures with straggly legs peep out from boxes and baskets, on the brink of a great adventure.

The article goes on to describe the bewildering noise and ...

> [the] voices of half a dozen languages. Russian, German and Yiddish were the main languages, but English was also heard. The area did a roaring trade as it could be a joyous day out – buying a pet and feasting on seafood, whelks, fritters and sandwiches in the jolly jostling crowd.

For some of today's older traders the market was the core of their trade and childhood memories; a day out to the dog market was fondly recollected as a family treat. Other sections of the community, however, might see the market very differently. In his book *Journey Through a Small Planet* the celebrated Anglo-Jewish writer Emanuel Litvinoff recalled his life growing up in the ghetto of Whitechapel in the 1930s.

He writes of visiting the pet market in Brick Lane and perhaps sums up the growing sense among some quarters of the public that the market was a place of cruelty: 'sad monkeys, parrots, mongrel puppies, neutered kittens, canaries doctored to make them sing sweeter were all on sale here every Sunday.'

In the late twentieth century the market, notorious owing to concerns over the welfare of the animals sold there, would fall victim to the moral standards of the day as society's attitudes toward the treatment of animals changed. The disquiet caused by the presence of birds and animals in Club Row started long before changes would be made in the 1970s and '80s, however. Newspaper reports from the early 1930s with headlines such as 'East End Market Scandal' and 'A Bird Slave Market' call for the practice of selling birds and animals to be made illegal. The reports highlight the way in which some birds were kept in paper bags or wooden boxes, hungry and thirsty, their plight as 'unendurable as the black hole of Calcutta'. The arguments put forward in the *East London Advertiser* ('A Bird Slave Market') were emotionally charged but showed that some members of the public were deeply concerned about the market and its treatment of birds in particular, to the extent that Lord Buckmaster would bring a bill to Parliament to address the problem.

The Protection of Birds Act of 1933, despite its flaws, certainly helped to safeguard wild birds, containing threats of prosecution for those who flouted the law, and had an impact on the sale of birds within Club Row. The Mayor of Bethnal Green hoped that the Act would put an end to the practice that caused, as the *East London Advertiser* put it: 'the name of Bethnal Green to stink in the nostrils of decent men and women.' Another politician and local councillor was equally pugnacious:

> ... he could not believe that a Borough of 110,000 could sit with folded arms while little feathered songsters were confined behind wires, deprived of everything that is precious in a little bird's life – their sight, sunlight, freedom, God's skies and God's fresh air – in order to gratify man's pleasure.

There were also calls made upon the local council to withdraw traders' licences 'at a stroke of a pen'; some were keen that the RSPCA should bring a fight against the slave treatment of the birds and drive 'the bird slave market of Bethnal Green out of existence'.

Although the days of birds on Club Row were numbered it certainly wasn't over for the animals, and 'the best bit of the market', as Charlie Burns put it, was to survive for another fifty years. The Act of 1933 did not extinguish the sale of birds on the market completely but spread the practice into the nooks and crannies, the hidden corners and bars of the market. Their sale thus remained in the market, furtively and illegally, for another twenty years. The traders engaged in it were, to animal lovers canvassed by the *East London Advertiser*, 'a monstrosity trading in cruelty; no better than slave traders'. These renegades and outlaws, impervious to the call to cease their trade, were once again set at odds with the authorities. In the 1950s the RSPCA and police made regular swoops in Bethnal Green and Club Row, finally responding to the public demand for action. It is worth noting, however, that the public outcry at the time did not deter many members of the public from keeping the trade going by purchasing the birds; the outrage was driven by a growing minority of interest groups.

The *Chronicle* reported in March 1950 that the police and RSPCA made their 'largest swoop of its kind for twenty years': linnets and goldfinches were taken and later freed in the open countryside. Such operations laid a foundation stone for the successful prosecution of traders and for moves to not only banish birds from the market but to end the trade in animals completely. The pubs that once sheltered the fugitive bird traders now feared the long arm of the law and posted signs declaring the prohibition of the sale of wild birds. The effect on the market was immediate; stalls and shops selling birdfeed shut down and another chapter was about to close in Brick Lane. In fact, by 1951 the call for improved animal welfare was being made in Parliament with the passing of the Pet Animals Act, which specified the conditions in which animals should be kept; however, it was widely believed that many traders flouted the law in this regard.

A newspaper article from the 1970s warns prospective customers when in Club Row to be careful of deceptive traders, who might sell you a three-legged dog. Those in doubt of the pedigree or health of the animal could turn to the RSPCA, who had an inspector on duty every Sunday. The demonstrators and the protests gathered pace in this decade: the traders in the 'dog market' were now in the dog house, out in the cold and distinctly out of public favour, and it became increasingly common for sellers to conceal their wares beneath their long coats, as they now faced a regular protesting presence and patrols from the RSPCA. The Victorian essence of the market still refused to bow down easily, however, with market-goers still making the choice to buy puppies, kittens, tortoises, fish and all manner of other animals.

By 1980 Club Row was entering an intense phase in its fight for preservation. Press reports of cruelty were gathering pace, with stories of traders abandoning unwanted animals after market closing and dead cats and dogs being found in bins. Radical animal rights groups were now demonstrating weekly against the trade, in what was proving to be a highly volatile and emotional atmosphere. The animal rights demonstrations were not always peaceful: the *East London Advertiser* reported in 1980 that two people were charged with obstructing the highway following a march against the market. The *East London Advertiser* reported on 11 July 1980 that activists were appalled at the 'inhumane conditions' and quoted one demonstrator on the state of the animals: 'Many are sick and are kept in tiny cages and die soon after being sold. The market is a relic of a bygone era, reminiscent of bull-baiting and cock fighting.' In some senses at least the connections to a 'bygone' era were, of course, quite accurate, but some of the allegations were perhaps unfair on most of the licensed traders, who tried to work within the regulations set down. At that time there were twenty-seven licensed traders in Club Row who were under threat of losing not only their licences but also their livelihood. However, it was not only licensed traders operating within the market: a continuing presence of 'illegal' traders selling animals helped to polarise opinion. Council officers found the problem difficult to deal with, as lone 'illegal' traders would be furnished with all kinds of excuses for being found with animals. They would often walk through the market with a single puppy or kitten tucked into their overcoats and, when approached, would have a ready excuse: 'I'm looking after it for a friend' or 'I'm waiting for my wife'.

These nuances clearly did not deter animal rights groups, who, radicalised by the whole concept of animals for sale, were determined to close the market. In fact, an RSPCA inspector was also quoted as saying that animals should not be sold within an open market. The *Evening Standard* had joined the call for

The bird mart, 1869. (Courtesy of Tower Hamlets Local History Library & Archives)

Animal seller, Sclater Street, 1956.
(Courtesy of Tower Hamlets Local History Library & Archives)

the market to be closed and, with the regular demonstrations being held by uncompromising animal rights organisations, the council was under intense pressure to react and submit to the call for closure. In 1980 Tower Hamlets Council met with animal welfare groups and the RSPCA to discuss the growing problem. The council, while recognising a crisis, felt

Jellied eel seller, Sclater Street, 1956.
(Courtesy of Tower Hamlets Local History Library & Archives)

Banana seller (possibly Johnny Bananas). (Courtesy of Phil Maxwell)

that existing traders were abiding by rules to provide adequate
conditions for animals, but the RSPCA disputed the claims and
were insistent that regulations were tightened up. Following the
meeting additional rules were brought in to stipulate that cages
should be kept clean and to stop people handling the pets to
prevent diseases from spreading. Enhanced regulations did not
satisfy the animal rights groups, however, who continued with
demonstrations and petitions. Overwhelming pressure was put
upon the council to revoke licences and shut the market to the
trade of animals. The end, it seemed, was now only a matter
of time. The council resisted for a short time but by 1982 they
had made the decision to close the market. Licences would be
revoked by July 1983. The end of Club Row as an animal market
marked the cutting of a significant tie with the past, 'the best bit
of the market' now consigned to history.

    There were still lone voices that supported the market, even
within the press. In an 'off the cuff' article in the *East London
Advertiser* in 1982 it was commented of the demonstrators:

> Their accents betray them. As with so many other issues in the
> East End they come from far and wide to lend support to whatever
> is currently controversial. Of course there are rogue traders: just as
> there are on many other stalls in this famous market. But in one fell
> swoop the council has condemned them all.

But there was no getting away from the fact that the council was
in step with public opinion in closing the market to the trade of
animals, and a colourful and troubled history was at an end.

Political unrest

The neighbourhood was afflicted with poverty and polarised by
race issues from an early date, in common with other parts of
the East End. The long history of poverty and political unrest

within Brick Lane is well documented. Views were strongly divided: in the early twentieth century laws such as the Aliens Act of 1905, seeking to restrict immigration, contrasted with the rise of political activism on the part of socialist and anarchist groups trying to further the rights of workers and improve living conditions, while tensions between the different communities contributed to the rise of extreme right politics. Groups opposing immigration, such as Mosley's fascists in the 1930s and the National Front in the 1970s and 1980s, were frightening racist, fascist and destructive presences within Brick Lane. Although they were finally beaten by anti-fascist campaigns, they left a distinct mark on the mental map of the area. Brick Lane market was quite often at the centre of those political battles and exchanges, as I will explore below.

Brick Lane's monuments are a clear reminder of the changing immigrant communities. On the corner of Brick Lane stands the Jamme Masjid, a Grade II listed building which, in previous incarnations, has been a French Huguenot chapel, a Methodist chapel and a synagogue. Next to the mosque now stands the most recent controversial architectural statement, the minaret tower, close by the Banglatown arch. However, the community that had the greatest historical impact on Brick Lane was the Jewish Russian community, which turned the street into, for all intents and purposes, the Jewish high street.

The area comprising Spitalfields, Whitechapel and Brick Lane, otherwise known, at various times, as Petty France, Little Jerusalem and Banglatown, was the place of settlement for many thousands of immigrants over many generations, offering freedom of speech, religious freedoms and better economic prospects. As described by Anne J. Kersher in her book *Strangers, Aliens and Asians*, the area of Brick Lane 'must have seemed if not the promised land then certainly the gateway to it'. All immigrant groups, be they Huguenot, Jew, Irish or Bangladeshi, shared a hard work ethic and a religious-based morality, and all would turn to the clothing industry and the markets for their survival and prospering. However, all new communities alike would have to suffer and fight for their existence on the streets of Brick Lane.

While many were demonstrating against cruelty to animals, a far more intense battle was being waged against racism on the streets of east London, and Brick Lane was once again the focus of attention. Tensions reached their height when Altab Ali, an Asian clothes worker who worked in Hanbury Street off Brick Lane, was attacked and killed by a group of racists by St Mary's Park in Whitechapel as he made his way home on 4 May 1978. The park was later renamed Altab Ali Park in his memory. That year was probably Brick Lane's most troubled, with numerous racist attacks, including this murder, which sparked many demonstrations and protests throughout east London and, in particular, in Brick Lane.

Racism within the East End has an extensive history, of course, and as far back as 1 May 1517, a day remembered as 'Evil May Day', there were riots against immigrant workers in Cheapside. In the sixteenth century it was not an Asian or black population under threat but one of Huguenots. Two centuries later Huguenots fought their masters and competing Irish weavers over wages and living conditions in the Spitalfields riots of 1736. Irish immigrants and buildings were targeted, resulting in damage to Irish taverns during violent clashes. The confrontations had race connotations, but were much more about securing living wages and suitable living conditions. Clashes between those in the weaving industry would decline along with the industry, but labour crusades and class awareness would continue.

The history of immigration has in general been one of accruing benefits to the wider community of London, but the new inhabitants suffered discrimination nonetheless. The Huguenots' skills in weaving did not exempt them from suffering bigotry and the Irish were no exception: Irish labourers, for example, helped to build Hawksmoor's Christ Church in Spitalfields, but their community confronted serious racism throughout its time in England. Jewish immigrants faced derision and racism when they settled in Brick Lane and Spitalfields in the late 1800s, although there were comparatively few attacks on Jewish immigrants in the area. By the 1970s the Jewish community had largely left Brick Lane for the suburbs and would be replaced by a new community from Bangladesh, which would also come under intense pressure from racists. The extreme right-wing politics of the 1970s and the forces in opposition to them had some of the most dramatic impacts on Brick Lane and the market since its beginnings. Brick Lane was to take Cable Street's place in the battle against racism and fascism.

The rise of the National Front and other racist groups, including skinheads, became a very visible sign of tension and right-wing extremism on Brick Lane. Skinheads made regular attacks on the Asian population of Brick Lane, propelling anti-fascist groups into action. By 1976 there were regular clashes between the racists and anti-fascist demonstrators. The National Front campaigned not just against the Asian population but also against black people, socialists and the remaining Jews in the area.

As the make-up of the general population of Brick Lane altered, the market, too, changed its ethnic identity. Jewish traders were replaced by Asian traders, and shops and restaurants that catered for the local Jewish population were now turning over to the Bengali cloth trade and curry houses. The bridge of the Old Truman Brewery, which spans Brick Lane roughly centrally along its length, was more than just a physical landmark; it also served to indicate the boundaries between ethnic populations: to the north of the bridge lay the larger 'white' population and to the south the incoming Bangladeshi population. It was at the most northern point of Brick Lane market, where it meets Bethnal Green Road, that a notorious stall in the 1970s would be at the centre of race wars.

The National Front and British National Party (BNP) had been escalating their presence within the market, selling newspapers not only in Brick Lane but in Cheshire Street outside the Carpenters Arms, the old stomping ground of the Kray twins. Their presence was exacerbated by their behaviour; it is reputed that they would swear and spit at passing Bengalis. It was in Brick Lane itself, however, where tension on the market grew around a newspaper pitch. The stall was held by a National Front supporter who sold books of an offensive racist nature alleging that the Holocaust was a myth and 'coloured people' should be put in cages. (The council was unaware of his political affiliations at the time of licensing.) Market inspectors reported that they had seen Martin Webster, the National Front deputy leader, using the stall, and concerns were soon raised that it was provoking more racist attacks. A wave of demonstrations followed against the 'Nazi' stallholder, demanding that he be removed from the market; the conflict even reached as far as the Trades Union Congress, where a resolution was made by Brian Nicholson of the General Workers' Union:

> Noting the attempts of the National Front to gain a base in east London and especially their provocative newspaper sales in Brick Lane, conference decides to initiate a mass demonstration based on labour and community organisations against the presence of the National Front particularly in Brick Lane.

The law made it difficult for the council to revoke the stallholder's licence, as licences at that time were revoked only for non-payment or charges of misconduct. But the growing Anti-Nazi League and similar organisations soon realised that if they arrived on the market earlier than him they could 'occupy' his pitch in protest and stop him from setting up. This action probably saved a protracted legal battle and national scandal for the council.

On the subject of racism, I spoke to Munir Ahmed, a market trader in Cheshire Street and owner of a prominent shop, 'Bashirs', on the junction of Cheshire Street and Brick Lane, for his recollections of racism within the market and the National Front:

Brick Lane used to be a hazardous area, where as a young boy it was too dangerous to come to in the evening. At that time [it was] still ninety-five per cent Jewish … but as they made their money and moved on the Asians moved in. [It was] dangerous because the fascists, 'NF', used to come down Brick Lane and harass people, shouting 'Pakis out' and throwing bricks at you. They weren't dangerous on market days, must have been having a day off, just handed out their fascist literature. Then there were demos against them and eventually they were driven out.

Munir than goes on to tell me an amusing and revealing story about racial tensions in Brick Lane, recalling the fascists in Brick Lane operating a shop in Bacon Street in the 1970s:

… run by … you know them boys with big boots and not much hair – ['Skinheads,' I say] … yeah, that's it, well it was a shop for all the skinhead fascists where they would get all their gear and that … well at one time the property round here was cheap and because of the trouble you could buy cheaply. Well, a Paki like me bought four houses half the going rate, one of which was this shop in Bacon Street. On the very day he bought it he went into the shop and spoke to the skinhead on the counter and introduced himself as the new landlord and [said] he would be collecting rent from him later in the week. The skinhead replied 'I ain't paying no Paki rent,' shut up the till and walked out and never came back.

Munir erupted with laughter and told me I must get that in my book. His sense of pride at someone getting one over the fascists was obvious, but he was equally joyful at the shock value of the story. And it is ironic indeed that the National Front, who were campaigning to get the 'Asians' out of Brick Lane, had helped through their actions to give the area such a poor reputation that property prices plummeted, giving Asians an opportunity to buy property and move in!

In 1978 a new police station opened in Brick Lane, staffed not only by uniformed officers but also by Bengali interpreters, in an attempt to overcome communication difficulties between police and the local community, to improve relations with the local community and to ensure better protection. The opening was met with some scepticism from the community, as the *Hackney Gazette* pointed out in November 1978, quoting Mr Golam Mustapha, a senior member of the Bengali community: 'We normally receive good co-operation from the senior officers in the force, but it is the policeman who comes into contact with our community at a local level who is the most important.'

Racial tensions and prejudice were very marked even within the market community, despite Munir's suggestion that the National Front did not cause much of a nuisance on market days. Racist attacks were frequent within the area, numbering into the hundreds. Asian men and women would be attacked on their way to market and shops by gangs of white racists, who drove around in cars looking for Pakistanis to beat up. Some abhorrent attitudes were also present among allegedly 'non-racist' white traders, as *The New Statesman and Society* reported in 1990. These views, I believe, were not prominent among the market traders of Brick Lane, as they had a collective sense of community support that had built up across the many different generations of immigrants into the market. Mr Bidder, the oldest trader in Brick Lane market, was quite candid about his views when asked about racial tensions. Shamefully, I had expected to find an underlying racist attitude in him, but the opposite was true. My presumptions were based on his age and background, but, as he comments:

> The market is a different world now than when I was a boy, really there was only one 'market' and that was Petticoat Lane. Brick Lane was the poor man's market, but now all the city people, 'hippies', come here. It was hard to get a living and even now you can't sell a great quantity of goods, you just make a bare living, but things have generally got better. See, in my day it wasn't multicultural, just Jews and English. It was [a] novelty seeing Indian people, now there's all nationalities [and] they're all grafters. I think it's better now. But I missed [the] market when I wasn't well. I don't do it for the money anymore, I just like the atmosphere.

The most important thing in this community was to subsist, and to survive extremely hard 'graft' was required. Respect was gained through hard work and mutual support, looking out for one another in a very tough environment. This seemed to override the worst of the racist attitudes that abounded within the market community, which, it must be said, is a credit to the vast majority of traders.

Although racial tensions did subside, it was certainly not the end of violence within Brick Lane. The Bengali street gangs of the 1990s, including the Brick Lane Massif, the East Boys, the Stepney Posse and the Cannon Street Gang, continued and embraced criminal activity in a similar way to elements of the older generations of immigrants who had also faced hostility. Gang crime was a time-honoured way in which to protect their neighbourhoods.

In 1997 further attempts were made within the Bengali community to secure their identity within Brick Lane with a controversial plan to install an arch welcoming visitors and community to 'Banglatown', a similar concept to that of Chinatown. The idea was not just a symbolic one but a serious attempt by businessmen to bring more jobs to the area and make the area of Brick Lane more friendly, to celebrate its history and cultural diversity. The Banglatown arch was erected in 1997, following controversy and opposition. The new identity symbolically placed on the area was progressive and positive, helping to redefine the Bangladeshi community as 'Banglatown', and the newly defined community celebrated with the Bangladeshi festival the Boishakhi Mela. This is the largest Bengali festival in Europe and is a strong unifying force for the districts around Brick Lane.

Race relations within Brick Lane took a grim turn on 24 April 1999 when on a busy Saturday afternoon a nail bomb exploded on Hanbury Street and caused mayhem, shock and terror within the community; thirteen people were injured. It is believed that the bomber, David Copeland, a former BNP member, had mistakenly timed his bomb for Saturday, believing it was a market day. Thankfully there were no fatalities but if he had been more competent the devastation on a Sunday would have been far crueller. In total, he planted three bombs across London in April 1999: on Hanbury Street, in Brixton market and in the Admiral Duncan pub in Soho, which tragically resulted in three deaths. They were a stark reminder of the extremes of racism and homophobic behaviour persisting in some parts of society. However, the attacks, rather than leaving a community divided, saw the various ethnic sections of that community pulling together to ensure that the community could lead a normal life. There was stronger police presence and additional CCTV cameras were installed to help monitor the area.

There are recent signs that the area still retains some tensions: in 2003 there was a possibly race-related firebomb attack by an Asian gang on the perceived white territory of The Pride of Spitalfields pub in Heneage Street, just off Brick Lane. Other motives for the attack, however, may have been the community's relationship with the police, as it was well known that the pub was frequented by local policeman; the bombing might be viewed as a precursor to the recent London riots of 2011.

However, the area has made significant strides in securing a more harmonious community. The yearly Mela festival goes from strength to strength in a reinvigorated community. This festival is revered locally, and has rivalled Notting Hill's carnival in recent years. It is a fantastic day for the market, restaurants and public. Brick Lane has slowly become the desirable area that local businessmen had wanted to create, with new businesses and restaurants (in fact, the area is now branded as the curry capital of London). But local Bangladeshis were not the only ones benefiting from the improved desirability of the area. A new middle class was moving in alongside property developers, changing Brick Lane into one of London's most trendy locations. The area is now going through perhaps one of its most significant changes – gentrification.

Gentrification and urban sophistication

Brick Lane can now claim to be the most fashionable street in perhaps the trendiest area of London – more cutting edge than Camden, Notting Hill and even Shoreditch, the area that it has now surpassed in terms of urban cool and chic. It is a popular tourist destination and the epicentre of cultural identity for the East End of London.

The journey from ghetto to shabby chic and urban cool has been long. The process of gentrification is one that many areas of London have undergone and that seems to develop alongside certain social and economic conditions. It is, perhaps significantly, Brick Lane's geographical situation which increases the strength of its appeal, though I particularly believe that the market and its beguiling history are the foundations of this renewed appeal and popularity.

The raw urban experience of Brick Lane and the theatre it creates has, of course, always been an attraction, but the area has never before seen the popular boom and mass appeal that it is experiencing today. This has had an enormous impact on the market, its traders, its residents and its visitors. In a series of talks and lectures entitled 'London in Peril', curated by Robert Elms at the Bishopsgate Institute, gentrification was described as perhaps 'the greatest peril that could be facing east London'. It is certainly true that the markets, not only in Brick Lane but also in Petticoat Lane, face their greatest challenges as well as opportunities.

The word 'gentrification' was coined in 1965 as a way to describe growing numbers of middle-class people moving into working-class neighbourhoods. Gentrification has happened not only in London but also in many other cities worldwide, in particular New York, where the Lower East Side has many parallels with the East End of London, having been home to new immigrants and renowned for its poverty. Another example of gentrification in London currently is King's Cross – and the success of this project remains to be seen. It could be argued that, as with King's Cross, gentrification involves the worst parts being torn down and replaced with something better – the nature of the 'improvements', however, is a matter of contention.

While in general these developments in London must be seen as of benefit, with the places concerned receiving a facelift and money pouring into the areas, I would argue that change, or gentrification, is not always an improvement, at least for the markets and the traditional communities that have used them. The property developers and big businesses are moving directly into the area. On the periphery of the city is 'the city of towers', which hovers on the horizon and quite literally casts a shadow over the area. It is a stark reminder of the power of money and business over local communities; its presence, looming over the Old Truman Brewery and the exquisite Huguenot houses of Brick Lane and Spitalfields, is dominant and demanding.

Broadway market, which has also seen gentrification, has seen the price of housing rise so steeply that very few people from the working-class communities indigenous to the area would be able to afford to live there. Brick Lane is in the process of following suit; the area is no longer the poor ghetto that it was, but is now becoming home to a very wealthy urban middle class. If it was not for the provision of social housing the area would now be entirely populated by the wealthy. Gentrified areas become polarised, with the wealthy inhabiting exclusive apartments and the poor trapped in council housing, while the middle-income earners flee to the suburbs or perhaps desert London altogether.

Like that of Shoreditch, Brick Lane's gentrification has not materialised overnight; in fact, the population of artists, designers, craftspeople and small businesses has in some ways expanded out from Shoreditch. As Shoreditch out-priced itself to small-scale artists and designers, opportunities dwindled and young artisans found refuge in the old Spitalfields market. Spitalfields was at first seen as an opportunity for change and development, but later, as rents increased within this area, the boho chic moved along to Brick Lane.

Spitalfields has undergone enormous change in the last ten years alone, swapping fruit boxes for artisan and vintage goods. In 2005, after a reputed £300 million regeneration and development programme, the old market was transformed into a chic fashionistas' shopping emporium, with new restaurants and retailers. Two new public spaces were created, Bishops Square and Crispin Place, and there was some restoration in surrounding historical streets. Although the Spitalfields development is tasteful and successful there has, since its regeneration, also been something lost: the area's cutting and gritty edge no longer remains. The area has a more commercial feel, connoting big business rather than small enterprise and local community. Chain restaurants overshadow the small food stalls and the fashions at times appear more conventional, geared towards the tourist market.

The flip side of this situation is that increased commercialisation has helped to put the area on the contemporary map. Where Brick Lane and Petticoat Lane were slowly becoming less relevant, the area is now awash with visitors and enthusiastic media coverage. It is certainly an area worth visiting, but with the caveat that an exploration of Brick Lane, as the more 'authentic' contemporary market, is all the more satisfying. Indeed, many stallholders from Spitalfields have left the market in favour of new private enterprises in Brick Lane, including the 'Upmarket', which rivals Spitalfields in size, and the 'Backyard' market, adjoining the Old Truman Brewery. Many other vintage stalls and markets have also emerged in the neighbouring area. However, it is not only the new private markets to which these stallholders have gone but also the market of old: the Brick Lane street market.

I attended a series of talks at Bishopsgate Institute in March 2012 entitled 'Chit Chats', during which I talked with three traders with connections to Spitalfields and Petticoat Lane market. One was Paul Gardner, whose shop in Commercial Street sells trader paraphernalia, particularly scales and paper bags. His family have owned the business since 1870 and have been selling to market stallholders through the good and the bad times. Paul commented that when Spitalfields ceased being a fruit market he thought he might have to call it a day; however, with the rise of small artisan traders business has picked up. He remarks: 'The area has regener-ated and the flagship is Brick Lane. It's gone like Carnaby Street: it's now one of the best markets in England. Look at the shops and stalls near the beigel shop, that's the best area.'

Transformation

Whoever has walked slowly down Brick Lane in the darkening air and
    a stiff little rain,
past the curry house with lascivious frescoes,
past the casual Sylheti sweet-shops and cafés
and the Huguenot silk attics of Fournier Street,
and the mosque that before was a synagogue and before that a chapel,
whoever has walked down that darkening tunnel of rich history
from Bethnal Green to Osborne Street at Aldgate,
past the sweat-shops at night and imams with hennaed hair,
and recalls the beigel-sellers on the pavements, windows candled to
    Friday night,
would know this street is a seamless cloth, this city, these people,
and would not suffocate ever from formlessness or abrupted memory,
would know rich history is the present before us,
laid out like a cloth – a cloth for the wearing – with bits of mirror and
    coloured stuff,
and can walk slowly down Brick Lane from end to seamless end,
looped in the air and the light of it, in the human lattice of it,
the blood and exhausted flesh of it, and the words grown bright with
    the body's belief,
and life to be fought for and never to be taken away.

('Brick Lane', by Stephen Watts: after the
death of Altab Ali, and for Bill Fishman)

Stephen Watts' poem, so evocative and eloquent, portrays
Brick Lane in all its colourful and troubled existence. In the
course of my ruminations on the changes in Brick Lane and the
surrounding area I came across his work and sought to discuss the
market and its history and present-day issues with him. Stephen
works as a poet-in-residence at Toynbee Hall and it was here
that he kindly agreed to meet me and share his thoughts. He is
tall and lean, with a great mop of extravagant grey hair that sets
him apart and reminded me of the stereotype of the eccentric
scientist – or, indeed, of the poet that he is. Rather than being
shy, he has a quiet but concentrated demeanour and is deeply
thoughtful about his beloved Whitechapel, an area with which
he says he feels a great affinity. Stephen's parents originate from
Switzerland and settled in the East End, giving him a real kinship
with migrants of all sorts. He recollected the market in the 1970s
and the killing of Altab Ali, and remembered marching to
Downing Street in demonstration. He said, 'It was a terrible thing,
but it changed things': the area would never be the same again.

Stephen comes to the subject of the markets as a local and a
customer (he tells me that his favourite market is Cheshire Street –
he loves all the bric-a-brac 'as you never knew what you
might find'), rather than a trader or an official, so although he
has few specific market memories he is nonetheless able to
offer valuable insights into the market and the transformation
of the surrounding area. He believes the area of Whitechapel is
becoming more homogenised and channelled: 'I feel as though
some of the area is getting closed off. You used to be able to walk
in diagonals, weaving from one place to the other; now somehow
they're closed off ... but I still love the area.' When I pressed
Stephen on these thoughts he clarified by saying that his views are
very personal to him, but he feels as though 'something is being
lost, although I recognise that homes have to be built'.

Stephen's thoughts chime with the undercurrent of the area's
transformation. The feeling of alteration was negligible over
swathes of time until the late twentieth century. The building of

huge office developments or new flats is obvious, but the more
subtle ways in which development and gentrification are changing
the area and how we respond to it are less transparent. Brick Lane
street market has been undergoing a quiet revolution over the
last ten years and the neighbourhood has slowly succumbed
to the drive of gentrification. New shops began opening in
Cheshire Street, overhauling the once dilapidated appearance with contemporary, quirky and charming independent
retailers such as Labour and Wait (now in Redchurch Street)
and Beyond Retro, and Taylor Taylor, an upmarket hair salon.
When Beyond Retro was established in 2002 on the junction
of Hare Marsh Street and Cheshire Street the contrast between
old Brick Lane and impending, gentrified Brick Lane was at
its most glaring, an emblem of what was to come. A few yards
away from Beyond Retro was tangible evidence for illegal street
traders, drunks, drug addicts and prostitutes, still pedalling their
'vintage' wares along the old school wall, the market inspectors
still engaged with moving them on. It is ironic that the age-old
illicit street traders were being replaced with glossy, licit versions
selling what appeared to the casual eye to be more or less the
same stock – and now it was young fashionistas who parted with
their money (usually considerable amounts) for battered old fur
coats, jeans, shoes and suits from a bygone age. The goods were
indeed vintage Brick Lane, but the contemporary street sellers
were a new breed.

As attractive as these new shops and galleries were, their
impact would soon be felt by longstanding traders. The new
shopkeepers began to grow impatient with street traders blocking
out their shops, accusing them of having a negative impact on
their businesses. Shopkeepers attempted to take street licences
close to their shops, leaving the pitches vacant, so that their shops
would be unobstructed from view. This, of course, impacted
negatively on stalls already struggling with a changing environment. Many moved to smaller enclaves within Brick Lane, either
on streets such as Sclater Street or in small private areas adjoining

Slater Street, where a tried and tested customer base was still eager to find traditional stall outlets. These stalls and outlets still survive and have an ongoing appeal to the many visitors to the market. On Cheshire Street the transforming market was becoming increasingly challenging for both the shops and traders as they struggled to adjust to harsh economic realities.

In 2007 I took the step of engaging with the shops and attempting to encourage some discourse between shops and street markets. This was encouraged by my manager, David Saunders, and both of us had a series of meetings with a number of shops to work towards positive solutions. Although some minor steps forward were made through the discourse unfortunately they were not continued, as other concerns and staffing issues took priority.

Cheshire Street, despite the influx of boutique retail, had been flatlining for years, and various problems have continued to impede the regeneration of other parts of the market. Gentrification has had a negative impact in this road but, conversely, so have underlying crime problems. The vans of market traders parked in the empty spaces left by pitch vacation became a cover for crime, in particular contraband tobacco and DVDs. The market became a woeful shadow of its former self, the market pitches suffering in comparison with the gloss of the new shops, and on every corner, it seemed, an illicit transaction was underway. As a result, the markets team, under the supervision of market manager Debbie Carpenter, took the difficult decision to remove all vehicles from the whole of Brick Lane. Traders had parked their vehicles close to their pitches for security and storage but, once they had gone, the market appeared liberated, and was opened up to view. The long-established 'Illegal Team' enforcement officers then moved in with a great deal of success, removing the unsavoury elements from the market. Cheshire Street is still lagging behind the other areas within Brick Lane market but is now starting to find its own equilibrium, with old stallholders adapting their stalls and selling a mixture of vintage goods and traditional bargain commodities, such as shoes and toys. Yet more shops have set up business selling high-end fashion and 'vintage' wear, for which there is ever-increasing demand.

Sclater Street and Brick Lane itself were beginning to change in a far more progressive way, but, if they were to endure they had to positively connect with the burgeoning success of Spitalfields market and the new 'Upmarket' by the Old Truman Brewery. The two areas were unnervingly set apart from each other, both geographically and socially, the contrast between the time-worn and modern hugely apparent. There was a great disparity between the old and the new markets in terms of social and cultural aspects and the class divide. The old cockneys and Bengalis were being supplanted not only by a new wave of East European immigrants but also by middle-class bohemians flashing their vintage pearl necklaces among the traditional traders.

An area of Brick Lane between the junctions with Pedley Street and Cheshire Street, where the new railway bridge now crosses, was underdeveloped but would prove to be the perfect seam between the markets of aged and new. The markets department made efforts to set up a legal flea market within the area and, as many of the traders came from poor and challenging backgrounds, the council relaxed some procedures to assist the experimental marketplace. Traders were charged a nominal £5 to trade, purchasing their tickets from parking machines, thus proving that they had made their contribution for a pitch. The market was managed with dedication by Toby Stephen Dixon, and the area attracted many traders and became remarkably vibrant. However, with the success came problems. Large numbers of traders wanted to work within the area, and disorderly, drunken and anti-social behaviour began to infiltrate the market, at times creating a very unpleasant atmosphere. Given the limited availability of staff and resources, the decision was taken to abandon the scheme and the flea market traders were ushered back to their original illegality on the fringes of the market, where they would be pursued indefinitely by the council's market team and the police.

The scheme did have some initial success in encouraging some traders to take up a full licence, however, and many of these traders helped the regeneration of Brick Lane. And more significantly, perhaps, the scheme proved that a link was vital between the old and new markets and that 'flea' traders were an intrinsic part of Brick Lane market. Traders within Cheshire Street in particular would be keen to see another attempt to bring back the flea traders, as they believe that their presence has a positive effect on custom and trade. Many licensed stallholders feel that without the flea traders the market will decline terminally and that they, too, will end up being removed from the area.

In 2008 I encouraged a new food trader to work on the edge of this area, and it soon became apparent that there was potential for a food court area. Chris Golds, the Market Administration and Development Officer, market officers and I thus worked to create a new food court area, again within the area of Brick Lane between Pedley Street and the beginning of the traditional street market at the junction of Cheshire Street, Sclater Street and Brick Lane. A more measured approach was developed on this occasion to guarantee traders in high-quality food with attractive stalls.

The new market soon became a trip around the globe, with Thai, Columbian, Turkish, Chinese, Spanish, Japanese, Argentinian, French and traditional English food all available. The council's competitive price and location also started attracting traders who had originally traded only within private markets such as Upmarket. One of the traders, Paul Undacath, added an interesting element to the new food court with the provision of a pleasant seating area and the board game Carrom.

The area has become a great success and is a dominant feature of the Brick Lane market trail. Significantly, it has had the desired effect of linking the new private areas around the Old Truman Brewery with the traditional street market. The effect within Brick Lane is startling, with the market now full once more. The stalls have developed with the times; more and more are selling 'vintage' clothing and cameras and other unusual commodities. There is still an air of the anarchic to the market, however, and I believe that this is its attraction. Surrounding shops sell high-end, quirky fashion, objets d'art and vintage goods. In 2012 the market is flourishing once more, its visitor numbers mirroring those seen in late Victorian and Edwardian photographs.

The appetite for expansion in the market now seems insatiable. North of Bethnal Green Road and west of Brick Lane is Redchurch Street. In 2008 this street was more or less derelict, with little to offer but boarded-up houses held together by ageing scaffolding. Its only apparent use was as a shortcut through to Shoreditch High Street or as an escape route for illegal DVD and tobacco traders being chased by police and market officers. However, the ongoing expansion of Brick Lane market has seen the street transformed into an artistic hub and quirky shopping destination. Its walls are covered with fascinating street art, of which that of the artist 'Malarky' stands out. In an interview with Street Art London www.streetartlondon.co.uk) he described his enthusiasm for street art and potential conflicts with authority:

> … as much as I hate to admit it, east London is also an awesome place to chill and go paint and way more people see the work, it's cool to paint there but it's been hammered so much you have to pull out something special to stand out, plus the police are real persistent round there.

Malarky's work makes a strong impact in the area, particularly in Redchurch Street, where his images vie for attention with new galleries, hip bars, restaurants, clubs and shops. In effect, the street has become Brick Lane Mark II. The area continues to attract an ever-expanding number of visitors, and locals are now outnumbered by young fashionistas and tourists armed with Rough Guide or Lonely Planet books.

I have also been privileged to have contributed to the artistic renaissance of the area; my works have been exhibited in the Real World Gallery in Hanbury Street in 2009 and displayed in perhaps the most beautiful of shops in the area, 123 Bethnal Green Road, now called 123 Boutique. These premises are just another piece of

Trader in Brick Lane, 2012. (Author's photo)

Brick Lane gent, 2012. (Author's photo)

proof that it is impossible to go anywhere in the East End without revealing another nugget of history: they were once occupied by gangsters and used to supply illegal guns. Now the building is transformed to a stunning showpiece voted by *Time Out* as one of the finest shops in London.

The expansion has not stopped here, however; at the edge of Sclater Street and Bethnal Green Road the place once the site of the dog market now gleams with the new overground station, in proud modernist concrete reminiscent of a giant Chillida sculpture, towering over the preserved viaduct arches. Poignantly, it is a reminder of former and contemporary developments.

The march of urban renewal has yet to eradicate all traces of the old streets, as the new poor retrace ancestral routes, eager to sell wares in the very same locations as their predecessors, triumphantly defying time.

5

TRADERS' TALES

The accounts below are first-hand testaments from traders relating their histories of life on the market. In my conversations with those people kind enough to give their time I used a similar question format throughout, asking, typically, how long they have worked on the market, where their family originates from, what their fondest memories are, how they see their relationships with authority and so on. Most traders spoke proudly about their lives and wanted to celebrate the market and their time as a trader, despite the inevitable 'ups and downs' and pitfalls that are characteristic of market life, and the main impression that I was left with was a sense of the freedom and joy that market trading and being part of London's street markets brought to those who worked in them.

Heritage traders

Tubby Isaacs
Tubby Isaacs' jellied eel stall is perhaps the most famous stall in Petticoat Lane and can be found on the junction of Goulston Street and Aldgate. It was first opened in 1919 by Tubby Isaacs and is now run by Paul Simpson, the fourth generation of

the family to have worked the stall. I interviewed Paul on a very cold day in February 2012, with London covered in heavy snow.

Paul has worked on the market for the last twenty-four years and, before him, his father ran the stall very successfully for many years. Prior to that the stall was run by Paul's father's Uncle Solly, who had been left the business by Mr Isaacs, who had left for America in 1939 because 'he didn't want his boys to fight in the war'. I asked Paul if he still enjoyed the business and working in Petticoat Lane; unfortunately, although he was good-humoured about his likely fate, he was down-hearted about the future:

> I like being my own businessman but it's not much fun standing outside in the cold seven days a week, nice in summer though … though I don't know how long I'll be standing outside for running the stall 'cause the council wants to get rid of [us] … all trailers moved for the Olympics, our stall is static and hasn't moved for eighteen years.

When I mentioned that I understood there were some issues about permanently placed trailers, Paul called for his stall to be celebrated and was upset at the council's seeming lack of interest in the historically interesting stalls:

> … we wished the council would do more to celebrate our stall; it's heritage and a tourist attraction. People come from all over the world just to look at my stall. I have film crews every month from one country or another filming us; they don't want to eat the eels but are fascinated by what we sell. I suppose it's like going to Spain and see[ing] them selling paella – you may not want to eat it but you like looking.

He went on to describe the decline in business over the years and his fears that no one would be taking over after him. 'If something has run its course it's run its course, but we should be celebrating it.' He felt that the big businesses could be ruthless in squeezing the small businessman and also cited the changing immigrant population as significant to his business, saying, 'Chinese [and]

Cypriots buy my seafood but the local Bangladeshis don't want it, maybe it goes against their religion, so that's a shame.'

Nevertheless, Paul related family memories of times when the stall was busy and attracted the 'villains and stars of the day ... Danny Kaye, Barbara Windsor, Burt Lancaster, Ronnie Corbett, Page Three models, the Krays, Jack Spot ... such nice people.'

Tubby Isaacs' stall is an East End institution that is celebrated around the world and it would be a significant loss if it were to close. I can only hope that it continues to serve the needs of a new century.

Louis Cohen

Louis Cohen is 73 years old and looks years younger; a slim and healthy-looking man, he tells me proudly that he has worked on the market for the last fifty years. Both his parents worked on Petticoat Lane. His father sold ties in the 1940s and 1950s and was known as 'Derek the tie king', and his mother sold ladies' fashion. Louis tells me that his family, like many others, had originated from Eastern Europe, his father from Russia and his mother from Poland.

I ask Louis about his favourite memories of the market:

> Without a doubt the heyday of the markets was the sixties, seventies and a bit of the eighties; they were good times, I loved being a market trader. The money was good and it was great meeting people; now it's just great meeting people, 'cause there's no money left.

It certainly seems that his generation of market traders could make a good living from their trade if they worked hard and played their cards right. I ask him how things have changed now:

> Well, everything's changed. At one time you would get coachloads of people to the market, but they don't come anymore, parking [restrictions have] had a devastating impact, then there's the Sunday shopping centres – they've helped kill things off. People have changed as well, I'm probably one of only three Jewish traders left now, but I suppose that's the way of things these days ... Oh, it was

so good in the day, you couldn't move in Petticoat Lane – droves of
people – and you had little offshoots to the market, like the gold and
silver market at Harrow Place.

Louis, transparently proud of the market, went on to describe
other traders who contributed to the atmosphere of the market
with their great variety of goods for sale, and mentions that the
auctions were a great draw to the market. I queried this, asking
whether the auctioneers were con artists, as I had supposed. 'Well,
some of them were, but there were genuine ones and people
loved them; they were great for the market but they were got rid
of, like so many things.' I sensed the old acrimony between the
traders and the authority rearing its head and enquire about his
relationship with the Tobys. 'Oh, they were alright but I suppose
one in ten of them was too much of a busybody or a wrong 'un,
but I got on alright with them.'

It was evident throughout our conversation that Louis Cohen
fondly remembered his years on the market and remains a proud
market trader of Petticoat Lane. Indeed, he finished by telling me
that he loved the market and 'will carry on working until I die on
the market'.

Alan Langley

I have known Alan for many years but have not spoken to him
particularly frequently, as he is a quiet, dignified man who tends
to his bike stall in Cygnet Street calmly and without undue fuss.
Without fail every Sunday he can be seen selling high-quality
bicycles to enthusiastic professional, amateur and child cyclists.
Ever-present on his pitch is his van, doubling up as a mobile
repair workshop.

Alan, who is now 69 years old, told me that he began on the
market when he was only 10 years old, in 1952. He used to do odd
jobs as a boy, trimming hedges in Stamford Hill, and was paid in
kind, in the form of a bike. He thought that it would be a good
idea to sell the bike in Brick Lane but was spotted by the police,

who thought that he couldn't possibly own such a nice bike and promptly arrested him. It was not until his father came to the police station and confirmed that he did indeed own the bike that he was released. Alan henceforth always traded in bikes and has always been in Brick Lane.

He recalled the market in Club Row:

> ... that bit was a wonderfully colourful market. The market sold every kind of animal: tortoises, canaries ... actually I had a relation who used to sell canaries and finches and bred them together, cross-breeding to make them better singers. There were some unscrupulous animal traders but no one would blatantly sell you a blind dog, but the animal rights people were the other extreme. The animal market made the lively atmosphere which made the market a place to come.

Seamen used to visit the market as well, bringing with them exotic animals such as monkeys and even lion cubs.

Alan went on to explain the history of Cheshire Street and Brick Lane, saying, of its villainous reputation: 'As they were chartered markets you had certain protection if you bought an item on the market between sunrise and sunset and if it turned out to be stolen you could not be nicked for receiving stolen goods.' Alan believes this is an ancient bye-law and similar to the practices of the antique market in Bermondsey. Although I have not found evidence to support his view it certainly adds to the myth of the market and its former reputation as the 'Thieves' Market', in which insalubrious activities were firmly entrenched.

The market's immigration history, even within living memory, was a subject Alan was well-versed in:

> When I was young it was mainly Russian Jews, then it was the Maltese and Cypriots; in the seventies the Pakistanis came. As you get the different immigrants coming in the market changes what it sells. For example, the Huguenots was tailoring and Brick Lane was Jewish with beigel shops, now it's all curry houses.

Pakistani sailors would frequent Alan's business in the 1950s and 1960s. 'They would come with a huge lorry and would buy up loads of bikes which would be shipped back to Pakistan.' In recent years, however, there has been a great influx of illegal bike traders and thieves who tend to congregate not far from Alan's pitch and that of Mr Petch, another bike trader of long-standing, probably to assume an appearance of legitimacy in order to fool the punters – but the police and market officers are not deceived, and continue to take action against such people wherever they appear.

John Calcutt

John's stall has literally been a cornerstone of Brick Lane market for as long as I can remember, and most certainly before I arrived on the markets. It is on the crook of Brick Lane and Cheshire Street and sells a variety of carpets and rugs in every imaginable design ever needed for a home. John is a quiet, unassuming but firm man who brings a relaxed attitude to his work. Always wearing his leather jacket, he sits cross-legged in a fold-out fishing chair, staring out into the market and watching the world go by or engaging in conversation with one or two of his friends that assist him at his pitch.

He recalled:

> Brick Lane was my second market and my bread and butter; when I started down here I was originally in Cheshire Street selling toys. That was when I was about 30, then after four years I got a transfer to Brick Lane, to where I am today, and started selling rugs.

'Nearly thirty-five years!' I exclaimed. John laughed:

> I remember when you first started, your first day down here: you were just a boy … I remember when the inspectors used to come around with a big brass bell at one p.m. when the market closed and getting reported once 'cause I was selling at five past one. The rent was only £8 then and I got fined £4. That was the only time I got into bother.

For John, the golden years of the market were the 1970s. He remembered the various characters:

> ... a trader selling circus ants in glass cages who got told off by the inspector, who told him he should be selling them in Club Row, not Brick Lane ... Ants! [I] also recall Prince Monolulu ... the market was jammed packed in those days. Things have changed now, for the worse, particularly with the economic situation, but there are still characters now, like Hogan.
>
> We had a forty-two-piece bone china dinner-set trader who would throw the whole set up in the air and holler in delight when the whole set was caught, it was quite a sight! Then there was a trader who actually used to print ten bob notes on the market and sell them. Another trader sold whisky, but when you got home you found it was nothing but vinegar.
>
> The market has always been like a family; we supported each other and had some laughs. I remember once, though, I was a bit naughty – there was a car parked in between my pitch and the one next door, well I moved the car and pushed it away but it got out of control and it went straight through the window of the shop behind us which in those days used to sell paint. I quietly walked away!
>
> It wasn't all good, however. The inspectors back then were bent and lots of money exchanged hands for good pitches, but you also took big money yourself then so you didn't mind paying, it was the done thing. The market worked then, but when they took away Club Row that's when it started going down and now, with the trendy shops that took over in Cheshire Street about ten years ago, they all pushed the traders out. Now look at Cheshire Street, it's dead. Herbert's fish stall [went], which was next to me, and they had been there donkeys' years. The market changed a lot then.

John is certainly right that Cheshire Street has declined, and he seemed genuinely upset at this, but he insisted that he loves the market and market life, although 'now I come out for [the] fun of it 'cause there's not much money in it ... The inspectors are all right nowadays and the market is still enjoyable but they need to improve the parking situation. It's dangerous with cars coming through the market.'

I asked him how long, at 69 years of age, he intends to carry on in the market. 'Well, my licence is up for renewal this year so I was thinking this may be my last year.' After a few thoughtful moments he continues: 'I think I'll carry on one more year.' The pull of the market is just too much for him to give up just yet.

Denise Brown

Denise has been trading on the market at the end of Cheshire Street for over twenty-five years, selling footwear and, more recently, antiques. She is an attractive woman, intelligent, unassuming and polite, and always appears happy to be on the market. When we spoke she told me that when she started she had an 8ft pitch, the only space left on the market:

> We sold 'seconds' and on our first day we sold eighty-four pairs of plastic shoes, we were overjoyed and were counting the money all the way back to the motorway near Luton! We were gobsmacked … we live in Northamptonshire and couldn't believe it … those shoes – cor, if the smell didn't get to you the sweat would!

She recalled the appearance of Cheshire Street when they started:

> Before the new flats that you see here it was just open ground, you had lots of traders selling anything and everything second-hand. … in Kerbela Street around the corner there were loads of rats as big as ferrets all over the place. You also had some strange characters about; I remember a man stripped to the waist carrying a meat cleaver in his hand [and] marching up and down the market, shouting out [that] he was looking for his boss, who he was going to do away with, and then there was this big fat woman who used to come down the market every Sunday, she used to go over to the record stall that was opposite us, the stallholder used to ask her to dance, which she would, then he would say 'show us your knickers' and … she would lift up her

big skirt and flash her knickers. The stallholder would then give her
fifty pence, but the funny thing [is] she did it to all the traders up and
down the market – she must have made quite a lot of money.

Denise, like others I spoke to, had a story about the Carpenters
Arms. I was expecting something about the Kray twins, but instead
she told me about its early morning licence, which all the traders
would take advantage of to get topped up with double vodkas first
thing in the morning.

It was pleasing to hear that she enjoyed life on the market, apart
from the early starts – but she liked talking to people, enjoyed
the company of other traders and got on well with the Tobys.
The problem now, she explained, was the demise of all the flea
market traders, which had had a negative impact on the market;
she would like to see something done to help bring them back,
and I attempted to reassure her that the markets team was looking
at ways to regenerate the market.

Nej Fehmi

Nej is, without doubt, the gentleman of the market, with a
presentable stall selling menswear in both Petticoat Lane and
Whitechapel. In all the years that I have worked on the market
Nej has always been helpful, hardworking, law-abiding and
thoughtful on market issues. I would speak to him frequently
regarding market issues and was delighted to hear him talk about
his time on the market and his family background.

Nej was born in Cyprus sixty years ago to a Turkish Cypriot family
and moved with them to England when he was 8 years old to flee
the ongoing 'troubles' in Cyprus. They settled in the heart of the
East End in Heneage Street, just off Brick Lane, and lived in a small
flat above a synagogue opposite the The Pride of Spitalfields public
house. Nej's father came initially, followed by the rest of the family
shortly after. The plan was always to return home, but the situation in
Cyprus deteriorated. His father found work on the Tube but died two
years later, leaving his mother to raise four boys on her own.

Nej observed that it was a daunting job for his mother to look
after four boys in a foreign country; living in the East End, she
was inevitably driven into the rag trade, finding work in a factory,
where she became a cutter. All of Nej's uncles had been traders
of some kind, either in property, auctions or antiques, and, living
so close to the markets, it soon 'got in my blood'. Nej laughed:
'I came from that kind of line but unfortunately I didn't inherit
anything.' Thus it was that he got started in the markets:

I felt helpless when I lost my father, it was very hard; but because
Petticoat Lane, Spitalfields and Brick Lane were so close – at
a walking distance – as a boy [I] would scavenge by helping stallholders. The market in those days … was such a hustle and bustle
you couldn't move, but of course in those days people couldn't afford
to go to shops, the marketplace was the only place you could afford.
I helped out at first in Spitalfields but then managed when I was
11 years old to get a job selling hot-dogs and ice cream in summer …
for someone that used boys like me, as we were cheap. I left school at
15 as I hated school and couldn't wait to work, and went straight into
a factory as a cutter and learnt the rag trade … at 18 I got a job as [a]
leather cutter in Leyden Street where they slaughtered the chickens;
Maltese people ran the chicken place.

I wanted to know when he first got his licence:

Well, in those days it was very hard to get a stall; it was like a closed
shop. So I worked on someone else's licence for a few years but
had to wait fourteen years to get a licence in my own name, which
was granted in 1994. In between time I had gone back to school
and studied at the London School of Fashion for four years, where
I learnt tailoring, which I loved, as I loved the trade. The market was
very tough but it was very busy, all the office girls used to come from
all over. Even mid-week in Wentworth Street an elite trader would
turn over £500 a day back in the seventies, that's why it was so hard
to get in …

Nej talked then about the make up of the market in those days:
'Although the market was 90 per cent Jewish there were a lot
of Maltese people, some Cypriots, Greeks and Turkish, mainly
people from the old British colonies – Jamaicans also, but the
Bangladeshis didn't really come until the seventies.' He told me
about the old Maltese men who used to sell gold illegally, with
rings on all their fingers and watches strapped on each arm.
I remembered these figures from when I first started in the job:
they were elderly men and usually dressed smartly in long overcoats and trilby hats, with shirt and pinned tie, but they would
gather surreptitiously on street corners to sell their wares. For some
reason we inspectors never really dealt with them, perhaps
because they were so artful that they could rarely be caught: as
you approached them sleeves would magically be rolled down
and hands put in pockets, evading attention. The Maltese, apparently, also ran the prostitution in Brick Lane.

> The Jewish traders all had a great sense of humour and were great
> at selling. Most of those old boys have now gone, but I remember
> as you would walk through the market you would see them selling
> to three or four people at once. A lot of traders from the seventies
> went on to become millionaires, paid for their children to go to
> private school and went on skiing holidays. A lot of these traders
> would graduate to become great businessmen and went into manu-
> facturing industries.
>
> You had to be quite hard to be on the market, a weak person
> wouldn't survive. It was and is a dog eat dog world; there was
> bullying, gangsters ... I remember my friend Eric, who survived
> [the] concentration camps, had to pay protection money[5] ...
> Anyway, when I got my licence it was on a good pitch on the corner
> of Goulston Street and I had trouble with the inspectors at the time,

5 I, too, remember Eric, who had died a few years before my conversation with
   Nej; the numbers tattooed on his wrist paid sad testament to his time in Nazi
   concentration camps.

one in particular, Sergio the Chilean they called him. I didn't know
the rules and he came up to my stall and started shouting at me, but
I bit back. After that he would send inspectors to my stall and try
and do me for petty rules but eventually he backed off. Nowadays
it's different. I get on well with the inspectors after they sorted out
the corruption.

The market in Petticoat Lane, though, started going downhill
when the Jews started leaving the market. They left when they had
made their money and in fact all the mainland Turkish traders that
are now on the market rented their stalls from the retiring Jewish
traders. Things further deteriorated when they changed the Sunday
trading hours [and] now we're facing the threat of 'online shopping',
but people love markets all over the world. Wherever people go they
head for the marketplace. In America, where they invented the mall,
it's killed communities.

I asked Nej what he thought could be done to save the market –
and if, indeed, it could be saved, and he said:

Well, the only thing saving Petticoat Lane at the moment are the
Nigerians, who actually have been shopping there from the seventies
when they got rich through gold, but really the authority has to start
again, wipe the slate clean. They shouldn't be afraid to try things, but
traders have to change as well; gone are the days when you could sell
rubbish – it all has to be a better standard.

[And Brick Lane] could be the next Camden. It's only 20 per cent
there now. Tower Hamlets have got this jewel but they don't know
what to do with it, [but] big money follows and already Gucci [and]
Prada are moving in …

Barry Sedler (Mr Kinky)

Barry was introduced to me by Nej, but I had been aware of him
for a number of years beforehand, as he is one of the 'old boys'
on the market. Unfortunately we have talked little over the years,
which is a shame, as he is an eccentrically charming personality.

When we met he was, I would deduce, in his late sixties, but I found myself rather embarrassed to ask such a personal question of this gentleman, who was, it was immediately apparent, a larger than life and unconventional character. Quite small in stature, he had blond hair and striking, intelligent eyes, and was highly animated, even restless, talking eloquently and at length. I realised as soon as we began to talk that he was quickly assessing my character to decide whether he liked and trusted me. Thankfully, it appeared that trust was reached, and Barry began to open up about his background:

> Fancy yourself as an author, do you? I should be writing a book, just about me and my life. I started on the market in 1902 [laughs]. Well, about 1970 anyway, selling shirts, dozens of boxes of them every day. It was good business. They called me Mr Kinky – years ago Mike Stern gave me a Napoleon hat and a pair of red knickers ... oh yes, I wore those on the market for two years, that's how I got my name. In those days there were some nice inspectors, but there were some naughty ones too.

Barry asked me how long I had worked as an inspector and was surprised by my answer, but then recalled the day I started, which took him back to his own early days on the market:

> Oh, so many memories of Petticoat Lane, I used to sell furs and had to have police protection, as all those animal rights people would stand next to my stall shouting 'murderer'. Those were the days. And Prince Monolulu shouting down the market, 'I've gotta horse, I've gotta horse'. [There were] other stallholders as well ... a trader called Walter ... always used to shout out 'Walter, Walter, take me to the altar', and another stallholder next to me used to sell spunky oranges – you know, mouldy – he used to row with everyone.

I said to Barry that I'd heard that he had another career in the film industry, and asked if he worked as an extra. Indignantly he responded:

Extra work, excuse me! I am a supporting artist in the film industry. That's why I came into the markets, to keep an income coming in while I was working part-time on films. That's why I just do the Sunday market. I've worked in dozens of films and went to the Toynbee drama school. I've worked with them all, Sean Connery, Michael Caine – they asked me to go into *EastEnders* but I refused.

On that note, his thoughts return to the market:

I knew all the villains: the Krays, they were gentlemen. The market's finished, you know – all people ask now when they come into the Lane is where is Spitalfields or Brick Lane, but I still enjoy it. I had Alan Sugar standing next to me once; he asked if he could work next to me. He was selling car aerials long before he started his Amstrad thing. The problem as well is the stallholders, they don't know how to talk anymore, all they say is 'Alright mate, 'ow you doin'?' – that's no way to talk to people. I can judge people within 2 minutes of meeting them and tell what sort of person they are, and I speak to them in the correct reciprocal manner. All right, if they're a thug I'll talk to them like reciprocally, like a thug.

At that, Barry wants to be on his way, and I thank him for his time, looking forward to hearing more about his extraordinary life.

Leonard (Lenny) Goldstein

Whatever the weather, rain or shine, it is certain that Lenny will be out working in Petticoat Lane. He has been a fixture on Wentworth Street for decades and is one of only a handful of Jewish traders that remain on the market. He sells good-quality ladies' fashion and has a loyal customer base. When I enquired into Lenny's time on the market he was enthusiastic to tell me his story:

I was born on the market; my parents used to bring me here in a pram and [I] was left by my parents' stall. My mother was born in England although her parents were originally from Poland and my father was

from Poland. In fact, most Jews were either from Russia or Poland ...
my father and both grandparents had stalls in Petticoat Lane dating back
to 1902, so my family has been on this market for over a hundred years.
I first got my licence I think when I was 17 or 18, whatever the legal age
was – I can't remember now. I'm 66 now and can remember the market
in the 1950s when it was so busy; [it] was like a family outing, it was
packed. The stallholders made a very good living for themselves, they
often made more money in one day than the average person in a week.

The market had different sections. Over in Strype Street it was all
tailoring and over in Wentworth Street it was 60 per cent fruit and
veg; you also had all the food shops, Mossy Marks and Kossoffs bakery.
You could buy beigels and herrings, it had a very Jewish atmosphere;
now it has a Pakistani atmosphere. It was tough though in those days;
if you were the biggest and strongest trader you got the best pitch.
That's why they brought in the inspectors, to sort things out, to keep
control, but they ended up taking over. Then there was problems
with the licences – it was first come first served, so deals were done to
get the best licences, but those days are long gone.

I barely needed to prompt Lenny, but I asked him about the
people he knew and the atmosphere on the market. He replied:

The market was full of characters. There was a bloke called the
'Colonel' who wore full battledress; he sold material remnants.
There were comedians on the market, Pearly Kings and Queens,
the Salvation Army would come, and people were just characters.
There was a bloke who just used to turn up at the market and tap
dance on a board, begging I suppose, another man used to have a
cigarette-rolling machine and roll out fivers. You could buy foot cures
and drink sarsaparilla. The market was, in fact, one big character.

Lenny came to life when recalling the 'old days', and quite obviously
still had an enormous amount of affection for the market, but he was
saddened by its downturn and said that it was 'only the Nigerians
that bought things anymore; without them we'd be in trouble.

The market needs improvements, somewhere to properly park your van, some advertising … but maybe things will pick up.'

Byron A. Thane

I have known Byron and his large family for as long as I have worked in street markets. For me, they have been synonymous with life within Petticoat Lane and Brick Lane for many years. The family have a somewhat infamous reputation as tough East Enders, but they are nonetheless hard grafters with likeable personalities. Byron, perhaps the most congenial member of the Thane family, had been perhaps a 'difficult' youth, but has now mellowed and matured, and is keen to work on the market without trouble. I arrange to meet him on a wet and dismal day in November at a café on the Hackney Road, and at once Byron is keen to recall his childhood:

What I will tell you is the absolute truth; these are my memories, my story. My parents grew up in the Guinness Trust just off Columbia Road – the Trust were good to people during the war. I was born on Columbia Flower Market on the Dalston estate; it was a big block of flats with a metal bannister that weaved down ten flights of stairs. We used to slide all the way down. If you fell, you fell ten storeys. We polished that bannister a great deal – the adults would shout at us when they caught us. Eventually they got workmen in to build bolts on the banister to stop us but instead we used to find bits of plywood and slide down the stairs. No money – we came from a poor family. When we were kids no one bought bikes, we had to find the parts and make them ourselves, but we loved it … or if the TV blew up you didn't replace it, you found the parts to repair it as it was too expensive … and we wanted sweets [so] we found many ways to steal them from the shops. Because you had nothing, everything was a bonus.

I've always been part of the market and remember going down Wheeler Street as a kid where they used to sell puppies. I got a dog on my tenth birthday for £1.50. I had him for sixteen years … [I] could speak to him, as he was more human than a human. He was called Butch, that doesn't sound very trendy now, does it?

He laughs, but his love for his dog is touching.

> When I was a youngster I used to rebel against the police as you
> used to get a clump from them, but as I got older I learnt to respect
> them more. I remember my dad telling me you can do what you
> like, but don't bring the police to our door. Once I was having a
> fumble with this bird in the flats, a policeman caught me and said
> 'Put her tits away' and gave me a backhand, I can see the funny
> side now [and] it put me on the right track ... they were proper
> cozzers then.
>
> This is making me remember so much ... around Columbia Road
> as a child I remember Mr and Mrs Jones, [a] Welsh family
> who had the dairy shop on the market which is still there today.
> Mrs Jones was a big fat woman and they were very strict but kindly.
> On Brick Lane I remember in the mid-seventies two brothers
> called Nobby and Dibble who worked outside the beigel shop.
> Dibble used to play the accordion and Nobby used to sell gold and
> diamond rings. Inside his waistcoat he had massive nappy pins with
> all the rings attached to keep them safe so he wouldn't get mugged;
> they were very rich. I started on the Petticoat Lane as a fly-pitcher
> selling knickers and socks when I was about 17. When it was very
> busy I used to love it, then it was shoulder to shoulder with people.
> You didn't have a lot of money, but it was a way of life. Doing the
> markets is a game of chance; you can earn no money, some money
> or lots of it, depending on who you know. There were some great
> characters on the market: I remember Lenny Rubin in Brick Lane
> who used to throw a whole tea service in the air and I don't know
> how he did it but it never broke. [He laughs] Maybe it was made of
> plastic or something.
>
> I did anything to survive, I bought everything slightly damaged,
> cloth and curtains which I bought in Dewsbury in Yorkshire, bought
> by the lorry load ... sold it on the market ... it did very well.

Hardly liking to interrupt his flow, at that point I asked Byron how
he got on with the inspectors:

I've seen so many over the years – it's quite a surreal thing when you talk to an inspector, but some are good now. I've done some bad things but I hope people respect me now. I'll always be on the markets unless the lottery numbers come up and I don't even play them! For me the markets haven't been work, it's like a dream that carries on … it's had its good times, very good times, and one or two bad times, but not many.

Byron apologised then, as he had an appointment to see a man in Stoke Newington about some gear, so I thanked him for his time and reflected on his generosity and charm. He epitomises the traditional trader, robust, savvy and, above all, a true survivor.

Fledglings

Brick Lane is at present far more vibrant than Petticoat Lane, and has had a larger influx of new traders. I spoke to some of them about their experiences.

Eva Koscielna and Andrloj Venkiewicz
This couple, genial and approachable, perfectly represent the new traders that have come to work in Brick Lane, giving the area a new appeal. Over approximately the last five years they have built up an intriguing stall selling unusual artefacts, often religious in nature – beautiful church icons and pictures of Christ and the Virgin Mary taken from redundant churches in Eastern Europe. They also specialise in quality modern literature. Andrloj is especially passionate about his books and exclaims with great exuberance when I show an interest in a particular book or author among his wares. His knowledge is second to none whoever the author and whatever the genre, and he can always entice customers into another purchase.

Andrloj told me that they had come over from Breslau in Poland approximately fifteen years ago. He was immediately attracted to Brick Lane, as it reminded him of his home city:

> ... the bricks, the smells, abandonment and neglect, streets full of
> marvellous records, ahh ... it was fantastic. I loved it so much I rented
> a room in Redchurch Street for twelve pounds and then in Brick Lane
> itself, above an off-licence on the junction of Sclater Street, but now,
> of course, it is too expensive to rent and I have to move further out to
> north London. The area just went boom ... and everything took off.

I asked Eva and Andrloj if they still enjoy working on the market
and how well they have settled. Both exclaimed that they loved
the market but missed their homeland: 'But you have to get on
with your life and improve yourself.' Andrloj explained his passion
for books, telling me that, back home, he was a bookshop owner
and has always treasured books. They also told me that they got on
well with other traders and with the inspectors, who are helpful,
'but we are always on time and abide by the rules ... but parking is
a big issue and is very difficult for the traders'.

This couple, with their unique stall that is part of the new
'vintage' scene now inextricably part of Brick Lane, are an asset to
the market, helping the area to regenerate.

Jerry Jerram

Jerry, an attractive lady, is another trader making up the new
breed of merchants that have turned Brick Lane into a wonderful
hotchpotch of interesting stalls. She specialises in all manner of
odd items, from quirky dolls to seventies memorabilia, but most
of her stock is comprised of paintings by largely unknown artists
from Victorian times to the present.

She is a relatively new trader and has been on the market for a
number of years, having previously worked in Portobello Road
market and Camden market. However, she got fed-up with how
those markets were run:

> ... there was very bad planning by the councils for those markets; for
> example, in Camden they turned the very successful 'Stables' market,
> which sold wonderful vintage items, into a bland area, building

Andrloj in Brick Lane, 2012. (Author's photo)

studios which now sell nothing interesting ... [just] cheap Chinese goods. All people do now is buy some food from their food huts and then go somewhere else; it's terrible. No one wants to buy vintage goods from posh studios.

I asked her if that's why she came to Brick Lane. 'Yes, but at first I didn't know why everyone said the vibe was great here ... it took me a while to get it. When I came about five years ago it was still building up, at first I thought it was a barren area, but slowly I built up my business.'

Jerry went on to describe her background and I was intrigued to learn that she had a degree in design and then only a few years ago retrained and took another degree in her passion, fine art, at the prestigious Chelsea College of Art and Design. She was forced to put her 'art' on hold while she built up her business but is happy at the moment, as her business, now concentrating on selling unusual paintings, has come full circle back to her passion.

She told me that she loves Brick Lane because it is different: 'It's not another Westfield or [a] boring shopping centre and is different from all other street markets; it is probably London's best street market. It works because there [are] not too many rules that can stifle a market.' An intelligent woman with a great appetite for life and for Brick Lane market, she hopes to continue to build up her business in Brick Lane and develop her art career.

Hogan Bennett

As John Calcutt pointed out (above), Hogan is a new character of the old order. Hogan Bennett has been on the Brick Lane scene for the last five years or so, selling bric-a-brac and antiques. He is an imposing figure: a tall black man who wears a long overcoat, sometimes with an extravagant scarf or cravat and usually with mirrored sunglasses hiding his eyes. When Hogan arrives on the market you certainly know about it. Hogan is quite obviously a cultured man, and talks as though he were educated at Eton and Cambridge. He is extremely charming and always entertaining, albeit eccentric. And he is certainly one of those distinctive characters upon whom Brick Lane depends for its unique appeal.

George Ozpembe and Terry Dervish

George and Terry cannot really be described as 'fledglings' nor as 'heritage' traders: they have worked on the market for approximately twenty years and are representative of the experienced stallholders that are the mainstay of the Petticoat Lane market.

I have grown up with both these traders over the last twenty years on the market and get on well with them. They are inseparable, and for as long as I have known them they have worked closely together, selling similar ranges of good-quality ladies' clothes. Both are animated characters who like to charm their female clientele, while in quiet periods they argue over issues related to football. George supports Liverpool and Terry Manchester United, and they endlessly bemoan and glorify their own team's losses and triumphs, particularly when the two teams play each other.

George is of Turkish origin and is full of a welcoming charm and comical banter; he is a hard-working trader. Terry's father, a Turkish Cypriot, came over to England in the mid-sixties and married his mother, who had made her way to England from Ireland. Terry proudly told me that he was born in the Salvation Hospital on Clapton roundabout and that he:

> ... started on the market when I left school and have made a fantastic living out of the market, but it's hard to maintain relationships 'cause you're always working weekends and long hours. There are lots of good times but it's hard in the winter – and, after all, it is the East End, so sometimes it's a bit rough, but I get on with most people, including the inspectors.

George, too, was keen to tell me his story, and suggested that if there was to be an extravagant book signing and champagne he would love to attend. I reassured him that that outcome is unlikely, but encouraged him to continue nonetheless:

I got started on the market twenty years ago. At the time I was studying business management at Greenwich University, where I ended up getting a 2:2. Well, I needed a bit of pocket money but when I finished my studies there was only poor jobs available, so I decided to do the market full time. The best times for me on the market were the mid-nineties, when I got my permanent licence. Both Terry and me work Petticoat Lane and Roman Road [alternately], and on Sundays I work Middlesex Street. The market's been good to me, I can't complain; I've made a good living and some of the characters down here are brilliant.

... the good characters down here were the old Jewish characters. You had Tony Katz and Lenny, of course. [Lenny Goldstein works a stall in Petticoat Lane between George and Terry.] Lenny would come out with some funny banter with the customers. I remember a large lady came up to his stall and asked for a size twenty-six. He asked, 'Would you like something in green and white stripes?' She replied that she didn't mind, then Lenny pointed to the stall's tarpaulin cover. [George laughs] Another woman asked for some trousers which were in white, and asked if they came in black. Lenny replied, 'If you turn off the lights they turn black.' He was full of them ... another woman asked for a size twenty and he says, 'You can take two size tens'.

As if on cue Terry approaches us, joining in with some banter of his own: '... I charm the ladies. If a customer asks for a size six I reply, "No ... no ... I can't, I've got a girlfriend." When they ask what I mean I reply I thought you were asking for sex.'

George's and Terry's stalls are too successful for them to be distracted by my questions for too long, and they are drawn back to their waiting customers. In parting, there is their usual flurry of banter about their expectation of wins in the weekend's football games.

Eddy Marciano
Eddy is one of the great eccentric characters of the market, and is certainly part of the new scene of Brick Lane. He is homeless in

the conventional sense, but has an extraordinary van, painted
outlandishly and with two gigantic model ears stuck on the sides,
in which he lives and works. Unfortunately, without a permanent
residence he cannot apply for a trader's licence, but he doesn't
let that stand in his way. Rather, he assists a friend who is fully
licensed, and together they sell an eclectic mix of second-hand
furniture and a peculiar assortment of odds and sods that he
collects during the week for preparation for Sunday trading.

Eddy's haunt is towards the top of Brick Lane, where he is a
dominant presence. He is an engaging and charming character,
revelling in banter with fur protesters and advertising his wares
(to the inspector's despair) through a loudhailer. I admire the
fact that he has overcome not only his homelessness but also
other disadvantages to provide himself with an income through
sheer hard work. He is polite and genuinely brings warmth to
the marketplace.

It is impossible to have a conversation with Eddy without
his telling at least one of the thousands of 'one-liner' jokes he
has memorised. When I first spoke to Eddy for the purposes of
this book he responded, true to form, with the self-deprecating:
'Someone wrote a book about me: *How I Murdered my Life*,' and
then quickly followed up with, 'I was on the motorway the other
day when I saw a sign: "Tiredness kills – take a break" and thought
to myself, even Kit-Kats are giving me death threats!' His gags
aren't to everyone's taste, but that last one had me chuckling.

Eddy's warmth and good humour were also evident on another
occasion – in fact, on the Queen's Diamond Jubilee weekend.
It was a very miserable, wet Sunday with very few traders working.
Eddy was out trading, however, and, oblivious to the weather, was
still commanding audiences with his presence and good humour.
I stopped to talk to him and noticed that, for once, he had objects
on his stall that could be described as genuine antiques – an old
Victorian mangle and a double Edwardian wardrobe, which,
somehow, he removed single-handedly from his van. Sensing that
he was in an appropriately jubilant mood, I commented that he

might get £100 for his mangle. Eddy laughed. 'No, I'll ask £350 for it. I just saw Gilbert and George this morning; they looked like they were interested.' An hour or so later I returned to Eddy's pitch and noticed that he had arranged a large amount of his goods in a big heap. He was obviously soliciting comments for his unusual stall set-up and so, continuing the art theme, I commented that his stall looked like a conceptual art exhibit. Eddy agreed, and said, 'Yes, it's my creation.' I asked what he had called it and, falling about laughing, he replied, 'Bollocks!'

Eddy's good humour made it a good deal easier to engage in conversation and enquire about his life, in the process discovering a more serious and thoughtful side to his character. Eddy said that he traded by fly-pitching a lot in the 1980s: the trade was extremely good, and almost anything could be sold. He told me that on one occasion a budgie had flown into his stall; he captured it and sold it half an hour later, claiming it to be a 'good talker but gets angry now and then'.

I wanted to know a little more about Eddy's life beyond the humorous banter, and asked him where he originated from. He paused and looked seriously at me, setting me up for a fall. 'My mother, I fell out of her womb.' After much laughter, however, he sobered up, and told me a more distressing story. He was born in Turkey and left many years ago because of the political situation. At the time torture was commonly used by the authorities, as Eddy experienced; he showed me some extensive scarring on his arm where, he said, an attempt was made to saw his arm off. He related this horrifying story matter-of-factly and quickly returned to the present: 'I just want to earn money so I can eat, but I do love it down here.' And, as if to prove the point, he is soon drawn away by other traders and customers, who take great delight in his constant stream of one thousand and one jokes.

6

REFORMATION

History reflected in its mirrors

'People want to reminisce in the old London and the hidden London ... '

John Berger

A lack of development or real investment within an area can have a devastating impact on local communities. Unfortunately one such area that has been left to languish is Petticoat Lane. The surrounding area has seen momentous changes, but Petticoat Lane lies forgotten, slowly eroding. Colossal corporate buildings have surrounded the area, casting their shadows upon it. However, it is far from clear, with the city in turmoil and building projects in disarray, which city skyline will best endure. As an appetite grows among the public for authentic heritage, there may yet be hope for Petticoat Lane. Even the men and women who work in the City, apparently distant and detached from those who serve them, seek out the marketplace as a welcome respite from soulless chain eateries; lunchtimes at the food court in Petticoat Lane are a mêlée, as the city workers enjoy the cornucopia of human contact

Petticoat Lane, 2012. (Author's photo)

it provides. The character of Petticoat Lane and Brick Lane is developing and changing before our eyes.

The markets are now frequently used as the backdrop to music videos and fashion shoots, TV dramas and films, such as the recent ITV series *Whitechapel*, which depicted copycat crimes rehashing the iniquitous past of the area, including the Kray twins and the Ripper murders, as if the original macabre events were somehow fashionable. I was once a point of contact for the markets department during the filming of the BBC drama *Luther* in Petticoat Lane. On a dreary mid-week day the market was reassembled for the convenience of the TV producers, the real stalls being replaced by authentic replicas to convey the desired market scene. The soap drama *EastEnders* is probably the most prominent television programme to utilise the markets, the researchers of the programme using them as the basis for some of their material; the drama, however, does little to reflect the true culture of the market, and particularly that aspect of it with which I am most familiar, the market inspector.

Aspects of the East End have become myths in themselves, the present parodying the past despite a setting stark against a pulsating modern metropolis. Similarly, the markets too are a time compendium, at once contemporary, yet reflecting their past. Brick Lane, Columbia Road, Whitechapel and Borough markets have successfully bridged the ages, but Petticoat Lane has yet to find its modern position and must provide more than an evocation of what went before if it is to prosper.

Corrupted legacy

In December 2011 a new shopping mall called Boxpark opened alongside the East London Line extension. Its USP is that it is formed from a series of container crates that house a 'mix of fashion and lifestyle brands' (www.boxpark.co.uk/about) – the first such 'pop-up' shopping mall in the world, and one that will be open for only four years, reflecting the dynamic nature of the East End. Adjacent to this there are plans for an arts hub, with support from Tower Hamlets Council. Lying between Boxpark and the future arts hub is Braithwaite Street, formerly Wheeler Street, in all its Victorian and gothic charm[6] – the street where I first ventured as a market inspector to pursue and close down illegal traders. It is now being primed for development as a new market area to further develop Brick Lane and to connect more closely with the neglected Petticoat Lane. The short distance between the markets via this street should make it an ideal link, but it must entice custom to be a success.

Once the proudest street market in the world, Petticoat Lane is struggling in the contemporary age. The market still runs daily, and more expansively on a Sunday, of course, but is a shadow of its former self. Visitors who have frequented Petticoat Lane for many years are now shocked by the great market's decline, often stopping to ask traders and inspectors the whereabouts of Spitalfields or Brick Lane markets so that they can visit them instead. During the week the market is sustained by a large African/Nigerian population who buy up large amounts of women's clothing and luggage to take abroad, where they make sizeable profits. It is sad to see market traders who have been working for decades persevere with the market, coming out in all weathers to battle for custom and a living. Sundays are better, but numbers are dwindling and Petticoat Lane no longer remains a 'must see' market for visitors.

There are some signs of improvement, however; a food court has been introduced in Goulston Street (as mentioned above), offering international cuisine and a pleasant seating area. Other imaginative initiatives, such as the partnership between Whitechapel Gallery and the council in a community project involving the market, its traders and its customers, are encouraging. And with promotion

---

6   The street was recently renamed in honour of John Braithwaite, one of the most influential men in British Rail history, who built the pointed arch viaduct for the first Shoreditch station.

for the market comes small shoots of recovery. Unlike Brick Lane and Spitalfields markets, Petticoat Lane has been hampered by a lack of investment and surrounding structural change; although the market sits in an enviable position close to the city, it is at present isolated from the development that is going on all around it. This geographical position could be its saving grace, however: how much longer can the area be ignored or left underdeveloped?

Recent developments concerning the fruit and wool exchange opposite Spitalfields show just how continuous new developments can be. The plan is to entirely revamp the building, leaving only the historic façade. In the process the remaining part of the building will be destroyed, along with the historic Gun public house. The scheme will create over 2,000 jobs, office space and a considerable amount of money for the Crossrail project. Planning was twice turned down by Tower Hamlets Council, but this decision was overturned by the Mayor of London, Boris Johnson, on 10 October 2012. The Spitalfields Trust, represented by the historian Dan Cruickshank, was at the council meeting when the decision was announced, and Cruickshank was quoted in *TNT* magazine as saying, 'The character of Spitalfields, which is special, characterised by small businesses, independent enterprises, is going to be seriously diluted and undermined and a historic street in a conservation area, Dorset Street, obliterated.' It is quite clear that development is inevitable in the area, however, and time will tell as to the consequences of change for the markets, as epitomised by the fruit and wool exchange.

On a far more modest level, Tower Hamlets' markets team sought to develop in their business strategy the idea of 'the Market Mile', a promotional concept consisting of a walk taking in the great markets in the vicinity and helping to publicise Petticoat Lane. The Market Mile would begin at Petticoat Lane and make its way through Spitalfields and Brick Lane before finishing in Columbia Road flower market.

Petticoat Lane and Brick Lane both retain an element of the vibrant, unpredictable, daring and enlivening places they have always been. Only now, in a new age of economic austerity, do the markets face an uncertain outlook. As far as Brick Lane is concerned, the tide of gentrification seems inevitable, but its unique charm rests upon its falling short of corporate take-over. Petticoat Lane, conversely, is in desperate need of investment and infrastructural improvements, but it, too, must strike the right balance to become a desirable market for the twenty-first century. It still has many remarkable traders dealing in exciting goods, and is still an interesting market to visit; with some honest reflection on the part of the traders relating to the commodities and services that they provide, and on the part of council in terms of the running and support of the market, much may be achieved, as there is still an immense pride in the market. But such change is not an option – it is a necessity. In short, the market must provide a little magic, something unpredictable, yet comforting in its familiarity.

'We are but shadows'

The Latin words *umbra sumus* ('we are but shadows') inscribed on the sundial set high up on the face of the former Huguenot chapel (now the mosque) are truly apt in describing the historical narrative of the markets and the transitory nature of both the Lanes and the people who have found their way to this small area of east London. The words have perhaps never been more profound, as the area faces its greatest challenge from the march of corporate power and gentrification.

The markets of Petticoat Lane and Brick Lane have survived through the years by being integral to their communities, crucial to subsistence in the East End and an important link for businesses, bringing stability to the area. Both have also been immensely popular with people from further afield, particularly, latterly, tourists. The challenge for these markets is enormous, as they now must struggle to prove their relevance in a world

in which modern gentrification stands side by side with older
elements that have remained constant in the East End: poverty
and extremism are still issues at times and in places, as changing
communities continue to strive for a peaceful and tolerable existence. The markets remain contentious in this sense, as they can be
an arena for petty crime and lawlessness: theft, prostitution, illegal
immigrants and assault are apparent. The legacy of Petticoat Lane
and Brick Lane markets has always been seen as somewhat out
of step with 'gentrification' or contemporary sensibilities: they
stubbornly refuse to succumb fully to refinement. In contrast,
Spitalfields and other historic markets have completed their transformation to idylls of moderation.

As this modern transformation occurs the local authority still
seeks to impose order, combating the crime that lingers within
the street markets and enforcing regulations as appropriate
while maintaining good relations with traders. The relationship between local authority and market trader will always be a
balancing act, as the former seeks to exert and impose regulations
upon the latter. The task of the authority is to ensure public safety
and balance the rights of 'stakeholders', including businesses and
residents. The trader seeks to redress the balance of power with
concessions on space and times to trade, areas to hold stalls and
the commodities that they can sell. In the twenty-first century it
is to be hoped that both trader and authority can work together
to develop the markets for their mutual benefit and the pride of
east London.

Recently I spoke to another longstanding businessman, John
Lopez from Brick Lane, who ruminated on the character of the
area. John has run a successful business in industrial furniture and
catering equipment in Bacon Street, next door to Charlie Burns'
premises, for the last twenty years. John knows Brick Lane very
well and told me he got started by renting his yard at no charge
from a character called the 'Sultan', in return for cleaning it.
His present lock-up contains an eccentric mix of industrial
catering furniture, antiques and other curios.

John mused on the changes going on in Brick Lane, particularly the development of 'vintage' retail and the dichotomy that this illustrates in Brick Lane: 'I knew a successful businesswoman who ran vintage shops in Camden who opened up in Brick Lane [prior to "vintage" establishing itself in Brick Lane]. She couldn't handle it, the locals just didn't get it; they don't understand "retro", they think it's just second-hand, and were always asking if she had a Hoover or a washing machine. The tourists understand, but not the locals.'

I think there is a truth to John's comments; there is a great deal of diversity in the attitudes of the people that now populate the neighbourhood, and Brick Lane remains at times a gritty area, not yet, as noted above, completely engulfed by 'gentrification'. As such, its appeal is wider than simply to those who would wish to refine and sanitise the area. This, in any case, is not such an easy task in an area such as Spitalfields; Brick Lane market itself (and indeed, Petticoat Lane) is 'vintage', but both the Lanes are commercial streets, and not lined with the elegant buildings seen in some other places in east London. The markets rely on the characters that trade on the Lanes to provide atmosphere and the grace and goodwill of the local community that allows them to continue. They also depend upon the intellectual and cultural stimuli within the area, in the form of galleries, writers, artists and so on, and upon its economic challenges and successes.

Brick Lane will only expand as the area's population swells and as modern links such as the East London Line draw more visitors to the area. The bohemian element is making the east the new west. Yet, despite these changes, the market not only survives but is thriving, its anarchic legacy still proving to be an enticement to the public.

However, while Brick Lane thrives, a lack of those elements that make it successful are proving a hindrance to Petticoat Lane: once the pride of London and 'the best market in the world', it is fighting for its continued existence. Although still to some degree an attraction, it can no longer fully compete as it did in its golden era of the 1970s, 1980s and 1990s. The traders are working in direct competition with big high street stores and its infra-structure pales against the gleam of neighbouring Spitalfields or Columbia Road. Both inhabitants and the sightseer find gratifica-tion on the alternative trail of trendy Upmarket, Brick Lane and Columbia Road markets.

The question is: does the market of Petticoat Lane have a future in a hostile and underdeveloped environment, before it is lost to the ebb and flow of the city and trading and shopping fashions move to new places? This is a plainly evident risk: as in so many other cases, distinct shopping areas of the past have been lost as new areas became the vanguard. At present, Broadway market in Hackney and Brick Lane are its representatives. I trust that a future is there for Petticoat Lane, but only if certain modifica-tions are made. Firstly the market has to be relevant and, in the modern era, also attractive in a defined way. But, as of old, it must also be a meaningful part of its locality, catering to society's needs. I believe it now must find its soul again and in our current difficult economic times this might mean a return to basic needs: the selling of second-hand goods in the style of a boot fair or 'rag fair'; the alternative, a gentrification of the market, would require substantial investment considering the competition that its neighbours would present. At present the market is still without basic provisions, such as toilets or cash machines, seating or pleasant spaces to linger. It does, however, have the advantages of its great location, in the heart of the East End, and the resolve of traders and others determined to push for a successful future.

When all things are considered, however, with the problems that these two historic markets face it is truly amazing that they still exist in the modern metropolis. The city ever expands upwards, with gleaming skyscrapers such as the Shard and the 'Gherkin' demanding their place on the extraordinary landscape of London's skyline. The Olympic village created a renewed interest in the heart of the city, in the pulse of the East End of London. All these grand projects could easily overshadow the shanty town below, with its life found in the crevices, but it still retains its fascination and need: it is in the street markets that people still wish to dwell, because they fulfil one of the basic functions that give the city its heart.

In a revaluation of the high street and markets in 2012 the government accepted the findings of Mary Portas ('Mary, Queen of Shops'), specifically dealing with removing barriers to trade. In addition, it promoted a national market day on 23 June 2012 and, supported by the British market authorities, a 'Love your Local Market' fortnight-long promotion that will be repeated in 2013. The report placed great importance on the concept of non-homogenised high streets capable of responding positively to community needs and regenerating declining regions. After the initial success, Mary Portas continues to push forward change and manage projects within the markets in Tower Hamlets, in particular Roman Road.

The impact of such initiatives indicates that there is a need and a deep-felt passion for the 'reality' and humanity found in street markets. As current economic conditions weigh particularly heavily on certain sections of the population the market has every reason to strive to continue: it could once more be an essential part of many people's leisure activities with the added bonus of affordable produce. As John Berger comments: 'I love street markets; I like them very much because buyers and sellers are still people, they haven't yet become servers and clients.'

BIBLIOGRAPHY

Archives
Bishopsgate Institute
British Library
London Metropolitan Archives
Museum of London
The Jewish Museum
The National Archives, Kew
Tower Hamlets Local History Library & Archives

Secondary sources
Ackroyd, Peter, *London: the Biography* (London: Vintage, 2001)
Beredetta, Mary, *The Streets of London: and How to Make Them Passable* (London, 1936)
Booth, Charles, *Labour and Life of the People. Vol. 1: East London*, including the *Descriptive Map of East End Poverty* (London: Macmillan, 1889)
Cooper, Jeremy, *The Complete Guide to London Antique Street Markets* (London: Thames & Hudson, 1974)
Davies, Andrew, *The East End Nobody Knows* (London: Macmillan, 1990)
Fishman, William J., *East End 1888: a Year in a London Borough Among the Labouring Poor* (Nottingham: Five Leaves Publications, 2005)
Forshaw, Alec and Bergström, Theo, *The Markets of London: a Complete Guide with Maps and Photographs* (Harmondsworth: Penguin, 1983)
German, Lindsey, and Rees, John, *A People's History of London* (London and New York: Verso, 2012)
Glinert, Ed, *East End Chronicles* (London: Penguin, 2006)
Harding, Arthur, *The Life of Arthur Harding: My Apprenticeship to Crime* (The Raphael Samuel Archive, Bishopsgate Institute, n.d.)
Hollingshead, John, *Ragged London in 1861* (London: Dent, 1986)
Inwood, Stephen, *Historic London: an Explorer's Guide* (London: Macmillan, 2008)

Jones, Owen, *Chavs: the Demonization of the Working Class* (London and
    New York: Verso, 2011)

Kershen, Anne J., *Strangers, Aliens and Asians: Huguenots, Jews and Bangladeshis
    in Spitalfields 1660–2000* (London and New York: Routledge, 2005)

Lichtenstein, Rachel, *On Brick Lane* (London: Penguin, 2007)

Litvinoff, Emanuel, *Journey Through a Small Planet* (London: Robin Clark Ltd, 1993)

London, Jack, *The People of the Abyss* (London, Macmillan, 1903)

Marriott, John, *Beyond the Tower: a History of East London* (New Haven, CT,
    and London: Yale University Press, 2011)

Mayhew, Henry, *London Labour and the London Poor* (London, 1851)

Munetsi, Mike, *A Guide to the Street Markets of London* (London: Freelance, 1995)

O'Neill, Gilda, *My East End: Memories of Life in Cockney London*
    (London: Penguin, 2000)

Partridge, Eric and Beale, Paul, *A Dictionary of Slang and Unconventional
    English: Colloquiums and Catchphrases* (London: Routledge, 2002)

Phillips, Watts, *The Wild Tribes of London* (London: Ward and Lock, 1855)

Rule, Fiona, *The Worst Street in London* (Hersham: Ian Allan, 2008)

Sinclair, Iain, *Ghost Milk* (London: Hamish Hamilton, 2011)

Sinclair, Iain, *Lud Heat* (Cheltenham: Skylight Press, 2012)

Weightman, Gavin and Humphries, Steve, *The Making of Modern London*
    (London: Ebury Press, 2007)

Wheeler, Elizabeth, *From Petticoat Lane to Rotten Row* (Manchester:
    John Heywood Ltd, 1901)

Wise, Sarah, *The Italian Boy: Murder and Grave-robbery in 1830s London*
    (London: Pimlico, 2005)

Zangwill, Israel, *Children of the Ghetto* (London: William Heinemann, 1892)

Websites

Bad News About Christianity: www.badnewsaboutchristianity.com

Bishopsgate Voices: www.bishopsgate.org.uk

Boxpark: www.boxpark.co.uk

East London History: www.eastlondonhistory.com

Gavin Kenning Engineering: www.market-stalls.co.uk

Jewish East End Celebration Society: www.jeecs.org.uk

Moving Here: www.movinghere.org.uk

Street Art London: www.streetartlondon.co.uk

The Universal Declaration of Human Rights: www.un.org

The Whitechapel Society 1888: www.whitechapelsociety.com

Tower Hamlets History On Line: www.mernick.org.uk

Tower Hamlets Local History Library & Archives: www.towerhamlets.gov.uk

Wikipedia: www.wikipedia.org

INDEX

Visit our website and discover thousands of other History Press books.
www.thehistorypress.co.uk